Parthenon

Power and Politics
on the Acropolis

Parthenon

Power and Politics on the Acropolis

David Stuttard

The British Museum

To my mother, Kate

David Stuttard has asserted the right to be identified
as the author of this work.

First published in 2013 by The British Museum Press
A division of The British Museum Company Ltd
38 Russell Square, London WC1B 3QQ
britishmuseum.org/publishing

This book was generously supported by
Philippe and Stephanie Camu.

ISBN 978-0-7141-2284-7

Designed by Bobby Birchall, Bobby&Co.
Printed and bound in China by
Toppan Leefung Printing Ltd

The papers used by the British Museum Press are
recyclable products and the manufacturing processes
are expected to conform to the environmental
regulations of the country of origin.

The majority of objects illustrated in this book are from
the collection of the British Museum. The registration
numbers for these objects are listed on page 240. You
can find out more about objects in all areas of the
British Museum's collection on the Museum's website
at britishmuseum.org.

Frontispiece Pheidias' statue of Athene Parthenos,
a serpent coiling at its feet, holds Victory in its
outstretched hand, while Athene's owl perches on
a Panathenaic amphora. Silver coin, minted in
Athens, 55–54 BC.

Contents

Preface

The Parthenon attracts the eye. Viewed from afar, it dominates the Athenian Acropolis. From close to, even in its present state as an artfully reconstructed ruin, it is breathtaking. Indeed, in the centuries since its construction, the Parthenon has become one of the world's most iconic buildings. Its silhouette epitomizes Greece. In the fifth century BC it was the proud embodiment of the power of Athens' empire, and of the politicians who had commissioned it, the artists and the artisans who had created it and the citizens who had fought to build the society it would come to symbolize. In later years, it underwent a series of metamorphoses. After the outlawing of paganism, the Parthenon was transformed in turn from temple to church to mosque to romantic ruin before finally, as a world heritage site, it acquired the status of a national (and global) treasure.

The architecture and sculptures of the Parthenon have been the subject of a great many books. In recent years, its afterlife – its changing function in the two and a half thousand years after it was built – has been increasingly well traced, too. But no book currently in print explores the circumstances behind the building of the Parthenon or the people involved in it within the context of the wider history of classical Athens. This volume seeks to do just that. By exploring the events that led up to the remarkable flurry of construction work of which the Parthenon was part, it seeks to set the temple squarely within Athenian history, religion and mythology, exploring how each impacted on the other and how all informed not only the Parthenon itself but other buildings both on the Acropolis and in wider Attica.

To help understand the building and its sculptures – the siting of the temple, the subject matter of its pediments and metopes and frieze, its relationship to other contemporary buildings of the Acropolis and Attica – the first section of this book looks at the history of Athens before the Parthenon was built. In the fifth century BC Athenians were becoming ever more aware of the importance of their past both as an explanation for the present and as propaganda, and in some respects the Parthenon is an expression of this awareness. Ignore this, look at the building in a vacuum, and we lose much of the meaning with which Pericles and Pheidias took such pains to imbue it.

The building work and sculptures of the Parthenon are the subject of the second section, which seeks to recreate the pride and wonder with which the project may have been greeted when it was under way – as well as the political jealousies and animus which it excited. But the Parthenon was not intended to stand alone. It was envisaged as part of an ambitious programme of religious and civic building, an embellishment of Athens and wider Attica, planned and for the most part executed under the governance of Pericles, the visionary helmsman of the city for over thirty years. In the final section, these buildings, too, are assessed against the background of plague, war and ultimate defeat.

Our knowledge of the fifth century BC, when many of the events recounted in this book take place, though relatively well documented, is sadly incomplete. At the same time, the Parthenon itself is mentioned in virtually no contemporary literature, and later classical visitors like the second-century-AD Pausanias were curiously reticent about describing or discussing it. In order to try to keep the narrative moving forward, I have inevitably been forced to compromise between giving enough detail for the story to make sense and saturating the text with too many caveats or technicalities. To take one example, much has been written about the so-called Panathenaic ship, a vessel which was somehow rolled through the streets of Athens from the Sacred Gate to the Acropolis as part of the Panathenaic Procession, and on which was hung like a sail the *peplos* or robe presented to Athene at the climax of the ceremony. Those who believe the Parthenon frieze somehow represents the Panathenaic Procession worry about the ship's absence from the sculptures; others argue that because of that absence the frieze cannot represent the procession. In addition, there is conflicting evidence for the late fifth century BC about whether the ship was part of the procession at all.[1] So, rather than get too bogged down in discussion, I have omitted reference to the ship from the text altogether, a decision I have been forced to make elsewhere with regard to certain other details for similar reasons.

Because this is a book about the *creation* of the Parthenon and its sculptures, much of what is now in ruins is occasionally described as if it were complete. For the most part, any imaginative reconstructions have been based on extant evidence, but the reader should be aware (as I am) that in certain cases our knowledge, like the artworks themselves, is fragmentary. For example, many of the metopes were deliberately defaced by Christians before suffering further in the explosion of 1687, when the Parthenon (then a Turkish arsenal) was blown up by a Venetian army. Many of the surviving sculptures of the west pediment were subsequently shattered when they were clumsily removed by the same Venetians shortly afterwards, so that the only visual records we possess are drawings made fortuitously a mere thirteen years earlier in 1674 by Jacques Carrey, possibly a Flemish draughtsman in the entourage of the French ambassador to the Ottoman Court, the Marquis de Nointel. Because of the resultant lack of well-preserved evidence, any reconstruction of what the Parthenon and its sculptures may originally have looked like and of what the temple *meant* to its first observers inevitably involves a mixture of archaeology, history and conjecture. Where appropriate, rather than include laboured discussions in the body of the text, I have flagged up such conjectures in the notes. ˎ

Similarly in order to return as far as possible to the mindset of the fifth century BC, I have tried where possible to remove much of the accreted varnish of centuries of theorising. For this reason the reader will find no reference to the so-called Golden Mean, a theory which is itself predicated on the notion that the Parthenon was built to an ideal geometrically predetermined set of properties. The reality is that (judging from the material artefact) the Parthenon was probably not conceived from a master plan at all, but – as with other temples – seems to have been made up as the work went on. Just as Aristotle's pronouncements on tragedy in his *Poetics*, based on his entirely personal judgement that Sophocles' *Oedipus the King* was the ideal play, can mislead modern students of Greek drama, so when it comes to fifth-century BC architecture the Golden Mean is a red herring.[2]

This, then, is meant to be a narrative, a story of people and events. By seeing the building in its context as a product of its age, we can, I hope, more clearly understand why it was made *as it was made*. Too much time has passed for us confidently to believe we can entirely appreciate the motivations of its creators, but by exploring the historical and spiritual landscape which inspired them we can perhaps begin to form an albeit imperfect picture.

Running like a continuous thread through the narrative –

or rather like the thin line of grey limestone which flanked the stone steps carrying the worshipper through the Propylaea and on to the Acropolis (see p. 184) – there is a theme of victory triumphing over disaster, of greatness emerging from defeat, of life returning after dying. As we shall see, this was the theme of the great Mysteries of Eleusis, which played a crucial and often unsung role in the concept of the Parthenon. It was the theme contained, too, in the great speech made by Pericles at the end of the first year of Athens' war with Sparta (and quoted at the

start of each chapter). The speech was delivered to the assembled citizens of Athens and their womenfolk on a winter morning shortly after the Parthenon itself was finally complete. And it is with Pericles, outside the walls of Athens at a time when the city's star was shining at its brightest, that our story will begin.

Below The Acropolis complete: an idealized reconstruction of the view from the west in Roman times. *Ideale Ansicht der Akropolis und des Areopag in Athens*. Leo von Klenze, Germany, 1846. Oil on canvas. 102.8 x 147.7 cm.

Prologue

> Our buildings and our monuments command respect; they are the legacy and the bequest of empire. In future generations men will marvel at us, as those who are alive today all marvel, too ...[3]

As the winter sun rose ever higher in the eastern sky, its new light bathing the city in an aura of supernal beauty, the rolling sentences infused their listeners with an ever-swelling sense of pride. Wave upon wave, the reassuring cadences washed over them:

> Our passion for the beautiful does not make us extravagant, nor does our love of culture make us weak. As for our wealth, we do not brag of it. Instead, we use it well, appropriately, for the good of all ...

The speaker had chosen his words carefully to inspire, to rouse, to raise the mood and turn what had begun some hours before as a solemn service of memorial to the dead into a celebration of the living, and a praise-song to the potential of their city.

The ceremony had started in the chill, dark hours before the dawn, when at last the signal had been given and the sombre procession

Opposite Athens' first citizen: the 'Olympian' Pericles. Marble portrait bust, Roman copy of an earlier Greek original. 2nd century BC. H. 58.42 cm.

made its way out of the city. Already and with due respect and tenderness, the burnt bones had been gathered from the tents in which they had been placed two days before, two days in which the families of the war dead had filed in to pay their personal respects and make their offerings. Now in the night these same remains had been gently laid in wagons, one for each of the ten tribes of Athens, and now they had been taken to their final resting place.

Behind the wagons, each drawn by a pair of horses, the clacking of their hooves like cymbals[4] loud in the silence of the crowd, there had come another, an eleventh, decked out in mourning like the rest. Empty of bones it may have been, but it was weighted with significance, a stark reminder that not all the dead had been recovered from the battlefields.

So, torches guttering, the mourners had made their way north, out from the Twin Tower Gate. They only had to go a little way, but all around them were memorials of death. For here, on either side of the wide road that led towards the grove called the Academy, stretched one of the city's cemeteries with its family tombs and gravestones.

A short way on, the first of the wagons had already reached its destination, and the biers had been slid off. Gradually the whole area around had filled with onlookers, a vast hushed crowd, the men of Athens joined for this sad ceremony by their wives and mothers, and by many of the foreigners who lived and worked here in the city. And they had been joined, too, by the widows of the fallen. For this was the national burial ground, the Demosion Sema, one of the most venerated settings in the whole of Attica, where only those who had sacrificed their lives in battle or had served their city gloriously might be laid to rest. It was generally agreed to be 'the loveliest of any place outside the city walls'.[5]

The ceremony had been observed with silence and solemnity. Centuries of legislation against extravagant behaviour at such

Above Tearing their hair, women mourn at the bier of a dead olive-crowned male relative. Red-figure *loutrophorus* (for ceremonial bath water). Attica, Greece, 430 BC. H. 67.8 cm.

funerals had seen to that. No wailing was permitted and no lamentation. Certainly no tearing of the clothes or hair. Instead, the cypress-wood coffins containing the cremated bones were lowered with hushed reverence down into the already excavated graves until side by side the war dead lay as side by side they had once fought, and the cold red soil of Attica was shovelled back around them.

It happened at the end of every winter, this public honouring, this act that linked the fallen of the months gone by with all those who had given up their lives in wars before, whether fighting as these men had fought against the Spartans and their allies, or falling far away in Egypt or in Asia, or preserving hard-won freedoms when the Persians came.

Only the men who died at Marathon were not buried here. For them, those few, whose bravery had entered legend, a special dispensation had been granted: their bodies lay together beneath a single grave mound on the battlefield, where they had died, while gravestones bore the name of each man and his tribe. For generations now each of the 192 men whose names were marked there had been honoured as the special saviours of their city.[6]

Now, though, at the national cemetery, now that the coffins had been covered with soil, a mood of defiant expectation gripped the crowd. It was the custom every year that one of their number should close proceedings with a speech, and this year that speech was to be made by the man who more than any other had dominated the politics of Athens for over thirty years.

Pericles, the head of the family of the Alcmaeonidae, himself the son of the war-hero Xanthippus, was known to his fellow citizens for his nobility and power as 'The Olympian'. Now he had taken his place on the high wooden platform which had been erected specially that he might be seen and heard by as many of those congregated there as possible. So, as the late winter sunrise stole across the sharply silhouetted eastern hills, and 'the patterns of the

vastness of the stars'[7] began once more to fade, the crowd, their
exhalations pluming in the still crisp air, had pulled their woollen
cloaks close round themselves against the cold and waited. This was
a voice the men knew and respected; many of the women, too, had
heard him speak, for this was not the first time Pericles had been
chosen to deliver the address for the war dead. But no one could
have known that the speech they were about to hear, marking the
end of the first year of what would be a long and devastating war,
would enter history.

For (at least as it was recorded by the historian Thucydides,
who like so many of his fellow countrymen was there and heard
it), Pericles' funeral oration encapsulated the values of Athenian
democracy and the aspirations of an epoch. In rolling, memorable
phrases it was a hymn to Athens and her people. Skilfully, it played
to the pride of its listeners and their forebears (even if certain of its
details were dubious to say the least):

> From one generation to the next until today, the same
> race of people has lived here in Attica, and by their
> bravery and virtue they have passed it on to us, a land
> of liberty. They all deserve our praise, but especially
> our fathers. For, they increased what they inherited;
> they added all the empire as it now exists, and, not
> shunning blood and toil, they passed it on to us …

Pericles went on to praise the city's way of life, reminding all his
listeners that

> we have many recreations for our spirits when our
> work is done: a calendar of public festivals and games;
> our private homes, refined and elegant; daily delights
> to drive away our cares. And Athens is so great that all

> the fruits of all the earth flow in to us, so that we have
> become accustomed to enjoy the best not only of our
> own land, but of every other land as well …

Pericles contrasted Athens, her politics and people, with her enemies
and rivals (and especially with Sparta), praising the city as a beacon of
civilization, as an 'education to all Greece'; and, although it mourned
the city's fallen, his speech glorified them, too, presenting their deaths
as a sacrifice made for the future greatness of Athens.

> They gave their lives for Athens and for all of us. Each
> one of them has earned a fame that will not fade, a
> resting place of such renown – not where their bodies
> lie, but where their reputation lives eternal in the
> minds of men, and in their words and in their deeds,
> as men for all time strive to be like them. For glorious
> men like them, the whole earth is their sepulchre. And
> their memorial is carved not only on a headstone by
> their home, but far away in foreign lands, unwritten,
> in the minds of every man …

It was more than a mere funeral oration. It was a manifesto,
which on that late winter's dawn was both immediate and
abiding: 'Fix your eyes each day upon your city, on her power,
on her success. And be her lover.'

While Pericles was speaking and the sun rose higher in the
sky, his audience, the citizens of Athens and their mothers,
wives and daughters, could see behind him their city coming
into sharper focus; and dominating the horizon, glistening and
gleaming on the high Acropolis, its sculptures glinting in the
morning light, the Parthenon, the building more than any
other which would become associated with the age of Pericles.

Above The grave-mound of the 192 Athenian dead at Marathon.

Many of those ideals contained in Pericles' oration might, in fact, be seen to be encapsulated in the Parthenon: ideals of courage and of sacrifice, of beauty and brilliance, of empire and democracy, of city love and Athens as a beacon for the world.

If, once the speech was over, any of the crowd now streaming back towards the city gates and the chorus of cockerels crowing in the backyards of the houses beyond them was contemplating anything apart from what they had just heard – or breakfast – they might have thought with wonder how all this had come

Above Courage, sacrifice, beauty and brilliance: horsemen from the north side of the Parthenon frieze. Marble relief, Athens, Greece, 438–432 BC.

to be. They might, with us, have sought to reflect upon the sometimes perilous history which had given rise to both Athens' greatness and the Parthenon itself, and consider what that building said about its time. But, in order to do so, they would have had to cast their minds back many years, to an age before democracy and empire, when Athens' character was only just being formed.

Part 1
Athens before the Parthenon

Chapter 1

Tabula Rasa

I shall speak first of our ancestors, for at a
time like this it is right and proper to pay
to them the honour of remembrance.[8]

ATHENS, AUGUST 514 BC

They were trying to marshal the procession when it happened.
A sudden knife blade flashing in the morning sun; a fountaining of
blood; confusion; shouting; one of the assassins quickly killed; the
other, running, chased by bodyguards through shocked and shoving
crowds; the victim's brother desperately calling for calm and order,
while expecting any moment that he too might be cut down, fearing
that in fact *he* all along was the intended target.

It was a shoddy killing, a botched job, yet, in the centuries which
followed, the murder of Hipparchus at the Great Panathenaic
Festival of 514 BC would be hailed almost universally as the seed
from which Athenian democracy would flower.

Above An early 19th-century sketchbook drawing of the Acropolis from
the south shows Athens in the context of the countryside around it. Sir
William Gell, 1801–1813. Paper. H. 22.8 cm; W. 127 cm.

The murdered Hipparchus and his brother Hippias, who had survived the deadly attack, were the sons of the charismatic and intelligent Peisistratus, a man who for many years until his death more than a decade before (527 BC) had been proud to be known as Athens' tyrant. At the time it was a term devoid of the pejorative overtones that cling to it today. In fact, subsequent generations would look back at Peisistratus' rule as fair and good, a regime that foreshadowed the constitutional governments of later years.[9]

Not that every would-be tyrant had been so esteemed. More than a century before Peisistratus had died, Cylon, the dashingly handsome victor of the two-stade race at the Olympic Games of 640 BC,[10] had tried to stage a coup. Eight years later, while many of the leading men of Athens were absent from the city at the Games, Cylon, backed by his co-conspirators, had seized the moment and occupied the Acropolis, for here was the seat of government.

A rocky outcrop some 3 hectares (30,000 square metres) in area, its cliffs rising to a height of nearly 500 feet (150 metres), the Acropolis dominated the town and undulating countryside around it. As long as anyone could remember, it had been associated with power: not just the power of men, but the power of the gods, too. And, standing on the Acropolis itself, it was easy to see why.

For one thing, it was a place of quite breathtaking beauty. Face north at dawn, and the rolling plains of Attica stretched far off in the morning haze, bounded in the distance by the slopes of Mount Pentelicon, while to the left the wrinkled folds of Mount Aegaleus emerged into the daylight from the purple bruise of shadow. To the right the pale blue peaks of Mount Hymettus glowed against the rising sun, while closer Lycabettus Hill rose conical and wooded, uncompromising and abrupt out from the stony plain.

Turn to the south, and there beyond the flatlands and the beaches, and the headlands and the bays, a short way distant was the sea, the coastline arcing round from Sounion far off to the south-east, round past the sands of Aixone,[11] past the bay of Phaleron, past Munychia and Zea with their shallow crescent coves, on by the basin of Piraeus, until, almost due west, the island of Salamis stretched rocky in the gulf behind Aegaleus. And out to sea another island, Aegina, rose dolphin-like, its hump-backed hills already catching the warm sun, while on the far horizon, the jagged mountains of the Peloponnese vanished like a dragon's spine far out into the blue mists and the south.

Placed like the hub of a great wheel between sea and rocky plain, the Acropolis (or so men would believe) was coveted even by the gods. Legend had it that early in Athens' history, when the grassy plateau of the Acropolis was home to a royal palace perched proudly on its northern flank, Poseidon, god of the sea, fought with Athene to decide which of them should own the land of Attica. There were many versions of the myth, and according to some the contest was decided with the help of Athens' first king, Cecrops.

> Poseidon was the first to come to Attica. He struck the Acropolis with his trident, creating the salt-water spring now called the 'Sea of Erechtheus'. Next came Athene. As witness of her appropriation of the land she called Cecrops, and she planted an olive tree, which you can still see in the sanctuary of Pandrosus. When the two gods fought for control of Attica, Zeus separated them and appointed the twelve gods as judges … Thanks to Cecrops' evidence that she had planted the olive tree, they awarded the land to Athene, who then named the city 'Athens' after herself.[12]

This account by the second-century BC mythographer Apollodorus may not be the most eloquent, but it is the most complete, and it introduces us both directly and indirectly to other characters closely

associated with the Acropolis, with whom we need to be familiar
if we are to understand the Parthenon and its associated buildings.
Unfortunately, it introduces us, too, to an example of the kind of
confusion that besets us whenever we try to discover any kind of
orthodoxy in Greek mythology. Thanks to both human creativity
and geographical variations, in ancient Greece there grew up a
multitude of stories about individual gods and heroes, some of
which contained elements of similarity, though many did not. To
complicate matters further, as time went by, 'academic' collectors
of myths (mythographers like Apollodorus) tried to rationalize the
different versions, blithely conflating characters and resolving what
they perceived as difficulties, until (paradoxically) they ended up
with accounts which were riddled with even more problems and
inconsistencies than before. Unhappily for us, these are often the
only complete versions of the legends to survive.

Which brings us to Erechtheus and his shadowy and even more
ancient *alter ego*, his suspiciously close namesake, Erichthonius, who
was himself connected intimately with both Athene and the Acropolis.
Theirs are stories which to us seem at once primitive and outlandish,
yet which profoundly influenced classical Athenian thought.

First, Erichthonius. Legend told of how, when Cecrops ruled
in Athens, the blacksmith god Hephaestus, having forged a set
of armour for his half-sister Athene, was seized with lust for her.
Eagerly he attempted to seduce her, and even when she rebuffed
him, he could not restrain his ardour, but ejaculated uncontrollably
onto her thigh. Athene, understandably somewhat taken aback,
sponged off the semen with a woollen cloth, which she then
threw on the ground. Nothing so far to put excessive strain on the
imagination. What happened next, though, was truly miraculous.
The semen impregnated Gaia, goddess of the earth, and in time she
gave birth to a son, a baby whose upper half was human, but who,
instead of lower limbs, possessed the body of a snake. (In mythology

Above Flanked by Zeus (l.), clutching thunderbolts, and winged Victory (r.), a helmeted Athene holds out a robe for Erechtheus as he is born from the earth. Red-figure *hydria* (water pot). Attica, Greece, 470–460 BC. H. 36.8 cm.

such prodigies are far from unusual: Cecrops himself was said by some to have possessed a similar form.)[13]

Athene, a virgin goddess not renowned for her maternal instincts, having first offered to look after the child, locked him in a box which she gave to the three daughters of King Cecrops, with the strictest of instructions not to open it. Naturally, this enflamed their curiosity, and when two of them raised the lid and looked inside, they went mad and threw themselves off the Acropolis. At some stage, Erichthonius himself seems to have split into two. As a human, he succeeded Cecrops as king of Attica, while his snake form slithered off to live on the Acropolis, where he was worshipped (and fed) as a serpent well into the fifth century BC and beyond.

As for Erechtheus, he too was said to have been born from earth; he too was cared for by Athene (though with greater tenderness than Erichthonius); and he too was to cause the death of Athenian princesses. According to legend, war had broken out between Athens and Eleusis, a city some 22 miles (30 km) to the west, on the other side of Mount Aegaleus, on the broad bay facing the island of Salamis. The somewhat dry Apollodorus again takes up the tale:

> When Erechtheus asked the oracle what the Athenians must do to win, the god replied that victory would be theirs if he put to death one of his daughters. When he had put the youngest to death, the other two killed themselves. It is said that they had sworn an oath between themselves to die together. In the ensuing battle, Erechtheus killed Eumolpus [king of Eleusis].[14]

The story of a warlike ruler brought by the gods to that unenviable place where he must choose to sacrifice his daughter to ensure his army's victory is common in legend. Typically, the ruler meets a violent end. Such is the case with Erechtheus. Eumolpus, the enemy king killed on the battlefield, was the son of Poseidon and it was only a matter of time before the sea god had unleashed his trident and Erechtheus, too, was dead.

Yet, for Athene and her city, Erechtheus and his family were heroes. Their deaths had been a sacrifice made for the future greatness of Athens, and throughout the classical age father and daughters were worshipped on the Acropolis, he with a shrine and an annual offering of bulls and rams, they with a heroine cult.

Looking back through time, the Athenians were to attribute to Erechtheus many of the rites and institutions which they held most dear. The annual Panathenaic (or All-Athenian) Festival, for example, culminated in the adornment of a *xoanon*, an ancient olive-wood statue of Athene, said to have been placed in her temple on the Acropolis by Erechtheus himself. According to the second-century AD traveller Pausanias, this 'most sacred of all the statues of the goddess' was believed not to have been created by human artists but to have fallen, already sculpted, from the sky.[15] Only Troy had boasted a statue like it, the famous Palladion, considered like its counterpart in Athens to have possessed powers to protect its city.

To the Acropolis, already magnetized with myth and magic, still other heroic legends were attracted. Like the stories of Theseus: how he had liberated Athens from her tribute to the king of Crete by offering himself as a potential sacrifice to the demented Minotaur; how when he had killed the beast, half man, half bull, he had sailed home in such excitement that he had forgotten to hoist the white sail which was to be his sign of victory; and how as a result, his father Aegeus, believing Theseus was dead, had thrown himself in despair off the Acropolis.[16] Other tales told of Theseus' many subsequent deeds of bravery: how he had abducted Antiope, the queen of the Amazons, athletic warrior women from the north; how the Amazons themselves had swooped on Athens and had threatened the Acropolis; how they had been manfully defeated

and Athens once more saved; how Theseus himself had died, an exile, pitched from the cliffs onto the rocks of Scyros, though whether it was murder or an accident, no one would ever know.[17]

Theseus was not the only king prepared to sacrifice himself for his city. During an invasion from the south, another, Codrus, learning from the oracle at Delphi that only his death would save Athens from defeat, disguised himself as a beggar, slipped out from the city gates and provoked a fight in which he knew he would be killed.[18]

The theme of heroic sacrifice for the greater good of Athens

Above Surrounded by depictions of some of his other labours, Theseus drags the dead Minotaur from the labyrinth. Red-figure *kylix* (a drinking-cup for wine). Attica, Greece, 440–430 BC. Diam. 33 cm.

permeated the city's psyche, yet the first time history takes over from mythology and we can place on the Acropolis a character whom we can say with any reasonable certainty did exist it is Cylon, the erstwhile Olympic champion, the leader of the coup d'état of 632 BC. But Cylon was ill fated. He and his supporters quickly found themselves beseiged. The Acropolis was surrounded, and in the searing August heat conditions soon became unbearable. According to the historian Thucydides,

> Cylon and his associates were suffering from starvation and thirst. Cylon himself managed to escape, along with his brother. But the rest, by now severely weakened, with some of them near death because of their starvation, sat as suppliants by the altar on the Acropolis. When they ... saw that they were dying there in the temple, the Athenians urged them to get to their feet, promising them that they would do them no injury. Then they led them out and killed them.[19]

Writing around AD 100, the biographer Plutarch puts a different twist on the story. He tells how the conspirators were persuaded to leave the Acropolis under the promise of a fair trial, but, in order to ensure that they remained under the protection of Athene,

> they tied a plaited rope to the statue of the goddess and held onto it tightly.[20] But on their descent, as they passed the shrine of the Furies, the rope broke of its own accord, at which [the authorities] rushed to arrest them, citing the breakage as evidence that Athene was refusing them the rights of supplication. Any who were outside the sacred precincts were stoned to death, while those who had sought safety at the altars were slaughtered there.[21]

It was an ugly episode from which the city did not quickly recover. For a long time afterwards, people swore the streets were haunted by ghostly apparitions, while the seers claimed that their sacrifices told of a city polluted and defiled. Megacles, the leading politician responsible for the atrocity, and his family, the Alcmaeonidae, were exiled from Athens, while the Alcmaeonid dead were disinterred, their bones flung far beyond the country's borders. But the Alcmaeonidae were not so easily got rid of. Like the ghosts of Cylon and his followers, the family will stalk the story of the Parthenon and the Acropolis until the very end. Yet in the century after the failed coup it was another powerful family that would dominate the Acropolis, a family which would cast a long and shifting shadow on the life of Athens: the family of Peisistratus.

Following the Cylon affair, tensions within Attica had continued to grow, until by the beginning of the sixth century BC it seemed that civil war might well erupt. With the passage of time,[22] the causes of this unrest have become unclear, but they appear to have had their roots in regional as well as class animosities. According to later sources, three sections of society were at loggerheads: the seafarers of the coastal strip, the conservative land owners of the Attic plain and 'those who lived around the hill', the strong-willed manufacturers and artisans of Athens itself.[23] Eventually, it seems the various factions agreed to entrust the reconciliation of their differences to one man, Solon. He was well qualified. Not only was he a wealthy shipping magnate, he was a general who had brought about the annexation of Salamis, and a philosopher with a penchant for writing poetry extolling his own virtue.

Solon's constitutional reforms became legendary. Thanks to the introduction of some clever compromises and judicious ambiguities in the wording of his legislation, he succeeded in strengthening the hand of landowning aristocrats while at the same time ensuring greater access to justice for the poor, bolstering their rights and cancelling their debts. Yet, even this was insufficient to bring lasting harmony, and by the middle of the sixth century, after two abortive attempts, Solon's own cousin Peisistratus (who, like Cylon before him, had been famous for his 'youthful good looks')[24] had seized power and declared himself tyrant of Athens.

Astute and ruthless, visionary and theatrical, flamboyant and manipulative, Peisistratus had already led a successful attack against the neighbouring city, Megara, which had been trying to stifle the Athenian economy by restricting trade (565 BC). Such had been the wave of popular support that, with the help of the grandson of the same Megacles who had overthrown Cylon two generations earlier, Peisistratus had gained mastery of the Acropolis and Athens (561 BC). It was not a situation to please everyone. Twice Peisistratus was forced into temporary exile, as rival families put aside their differences and rose against him. But from his final return in 546 BC until his death almost twenty years later (527 BC), Peisistratus imposed his relatively benign tyranny on Athens and set about raising his city's profile.

Even as Peisistratus was consolidating his power base in the 560s BC, a brave new temple to Athene had been raised in the southern quadrant of the Acropolis. Perched high above the city and built of limestone, it encapsulated the spirit of its age, for, in the sixth century BC across the sea lanes of the Mediterranean and the Aegean, Greek cities with pretensions to an international reputation were competing to enhance their sanctuaries and shrines with new-style colonnaded temples, houses for their gods, homes for their gods' statues, status symbols for the tyrants who had built them. The sheer cost of temple building was enormous. The investment in not only raw materials and personnel but in time, too, was huge, while the logistics of project management were second only to those seen on complex military campaigns. But, for the kudos which the finished structure brought, and for the prestige accumulated by its

sponsor, whether individual or family or wider civic group, they were well worth it.

This limestone temple of Athene was no exception. Not only was the building itself magnificent, but no expense was spared to adorn it with brightly painted sculptures showing not only creatures from mythology like a three-headed male figure whose triform body ended in a coiled snake's tail, but those most aristocratic of creatures, lions, mauling a stricken deer.

Later, under Peisistratus' rule, a sturdy entrance gate or Propylaea was erected at the west of the Acropolis, the only way onto the rock. From now on, even more than ever, the Acropolis became a segregated space, a place to which access could be carefully controlled, a zone not only of religious exclusivity but (if the situation should arise) of increased military security as well.

Now, throughout Athens, further building work would follow. Within the boundaries of the increasingly prosperous city, in a prestigious area south-east of the Acropolis close by the River Ilissos, a temple to Olympian Zeus was raised, while to the north-west an aqueduct was built to feed a fountain of bubbling water

Above The three-headed male figure with coiled snake tail from Athene's limestone temple still bears traces of original paint.

that would provide Athenians with cool relief in the baking bustle of their marketplace, the Agora.

At the same time, Peisistratus was determined that Athens should compete with her most prestigious rivals. In the decades before he had come to power, new athletic festivals to challenge the Olympic Games had sprung up at Delphi, Corinth and Nemea. To Peisistratus they cried out to be augmented by a fifth. So, taking as his model the annual Panathenaic Festival (inaugurated, so it was claimed, by King Erechtheus), he created a new and vastly more magnificent event, the so-called *Great* Panathenaic Festival, celebrated like the others every four years, a heady mix of sporting contests, sacrifices and processions, all woven round the ancient ceremony of the presentation of a sacred robe (or *peplos*) to the 'heaven sent' *xoanon*, the olive-wood statue of Athene on the Acropolis.

At the newly annexed town of Eleusis, too, where the fertile plain met the sea across the straits from Salamis, Peisistratus took control of the so-called Mysteries of Demeter and Persephone. These involved a series of initiation ceremonies, at whose heart were rituals re-enacting the great cycles of death and rebirth, which mirrored myths surrounding the two harvest goddesses. When her daughter Persephone was abducted by Hades, god of the dead, and taken with him to the Underworld, Demeter, goddess of the earth's fertility, was distraught. As she shrivelled in her grief, so the earth shrivelled too, until, with the world almost destroyed by famine, Zeus intervened. Hades agreed to return Persephone to her mother on condition that the girl had eaten nothing during her stay with him. But eaten she had: a handful of pomegranate seeds. So, although mother and daughter were reunited, every year for a period of months Persephone had to return to the Underworld, and every year Demeter grieved for her loss; and during the period of her grief, in the scorching height of summer, the earth baked and withered and nothing grew. But with Persephone's return came lush fertility.

Legend told how, as she wandered the earth in search of her daughter, Demeter had been treated kindly by the king of Eleusis and, in gratitude, she had taught his son Triptolemus the arts of agriculture and the secrets of nature, secrets which were then passed on to those initiated into the Mysteries. So each September[25] for 1000 years a procession wound its way from Athens' 'Sacred Gate' out through the olive groves and vineyards, across the foothills of Aegaleus, and down to the rocky outcrop at Eleusis, surrounded by a sea of wheat fields, to celebrate the cycles of death and of rebirth.

The Great Panathenaia and the Mysteries were not the only civic celebrations boosted by Peisistratus. During his rule, a new art form had been invented. On the wooded slopes of Mount Pentelicon at the village of Icaria (modern Ekali), in the annual festival of choral singing sacred to Dionysus, god of metamorphosis and wine, a performer, Thespis, had somehow slipped into the role of one of the song's characters and so become the western world's first actor. Such was the universal enthusiasm with which drama was greeted that in 534 BC Peisistratus instituted the first City Dionysia in Athens, part arts event, part religious ceremony and part civic competition, in which rival playwrights clashed to see whose work might be most popular.

Nor was drama the only literary genre whose potential power was harnessed by Peisistratus. The epic poems attributed to Homer, and most especially the *Iliad* and *Odyssey*, had long been common currency among Greek speakers. But, like myths, they existed in many different forms, the product of centuries of oral retelling. Now Peisistratus, in a further bid to make Athens the cultural capital of the Greek world, gathered a team of experts, scholars and poets and, in a quite unprecedented act, sought to fashion one canonical version of the Homeric text. In doing so, he had an eye not just for literature, but for politics, too. According to Plutarch,

> he inserted into Homer's *Book of the Dead* [Odyssey 11] the line, 'Theseus and Peirithous, famed sons of heaven', simply to please the Athenians.[26]

In fact, there was more to it than that. For, at a time when the works of Homer were commonly consulted in order to resolve international disputes, thanks to careful manipulation, additions and subtractions, Peisistratus succeeded in 'finding' certain lines which were beneficial to Athenian interests, while 'losing' others which were not. The power of art as propaganda had been discovered.

It was a time of boundless possibilities. Standing on the Acropolis at the heart of his regenerated city, Peisistratus could gaze down at the bustling Agora, across the busy warren of Athens' streets and houses where smoke rose from the furnaces of metalworkers and from potters' kilns, out past the city walls to the well-tilled fields on one side and on the other to the sea, white with the sails of merchant ships which plied their way to the thousand other cities of the Greek world and beyond. And he could feel, quite rightly, proud.

For he had achieved his purpose. He had put Athens on the map.

Such was his success that on his death in 527 BC his rule passed uncontested to Hippias, his elder son. Together with his brother, Hipparchus, Hippias sought to continue Peisistratus' policies, and not least in the sphere of temple building. Assembling a skilled team of architects, they inaugurated their own ambitious construction programme. By the banks of the Ilissus, work began on a new temple to Olympian Zeus, greater by far than that built by their father. On a platform measuring some 350 by 135 feet (108 by 41 metres) craftsmen started to lay out the bases for a double colonnade of towering columns, eight on the two short sides, twenty-one on the long flanks. It was to be the biggest and the grandest temple on mainland Greece.

For the brothers had heard reports of two great temples in the
east, or perhaps they had seen them themselves – one on Samos, built
in honour of the goddess Hera by Polycrates (a tyrant every bit as
energetic and as innovative as Peisistratus had been), the other, the
stunningly beautiful temple to Artemis on the azure coast at Ephesus.
It, too, had a double colonnade, and its columns were elaborately
sculpted with figures in procession: men, some with long flowing hair
and draped in panther skins; women with full lips and almond eyes;
horses; cattle driven to the altar to be sacrificed. And on the frieze
above them, more processions, chariots and horses, figures seated
in assembly; and interspersed with these were scenes from legend:
battles between humans and the half-man half-horse centaurs; battles
with Amazons; and strange beasts, lions and oxen.[27] The Artemision

Above From the early temple of Artemis at Ephesus, a fragmentary
sculpture shows a young man holding his horse's reins. Athens, Greece,
late 6th/early 5th century BC. H. 16 cm; L. 19 cm.

was quite simply the most stunning building anywhere in the Greek world. But it had been funded in part by a foreigner, Croesus, the supremely wealthy king of Lydia. And now, in Athens, by the banks of the Ilissos, financed purely from their own resources, Hippias and Hipparchus meant to surpass it.

On the Acropolis, too, amid a blossoming of shrines and precincts sacred not only to the city's patron goddess but to others, such as Artemis and Zeus, just to the north of the temple which Peisistratus had built, and angled parallel to it, they set their architects to work on a new temple to Athene Polias (Athene who Protects the City). Look up at its pediments, and you would see breathtaking sculptures showing the legendary victory of the gods over the giants, primeval forces of destruction who had sought to overthrow the rule of law and justice and to plunge the world into chaotic ruin. And at the heart of the conflict, wielding her spear and shaking her snake-fringed *aegis*, her goat-skin breast-plate adorned with the terrifying Gorgon's head, was Athene herself in all her majesty and her protective power.

The subject matter of these sculptures was appropriate. For the temple was to house that most potent statue of Athene, the olive-wood *xoanon* first dedicated by Erechtheus, and clothed each year in its new robe. And each year on that robe was woven, by young girls chosen from the best and richest families of Athenian aristocracy, the same scene as the pedimental sculptures showed: the battle of the gods and giants. How ironic, then, that it was this robe which, in part, would cause the downfall of the family of Peisistratus.

To be chosen to help weave the robe was something to which every young well-born Athenian girl aspired. Every August at the start of the Athenian new year, four of them, each between seven and ten years old, would be picked to be so-called Arrephoroi, removed from their family homes and taken with a group of older girls, the Ergastinai, to live in a special house built at the north-west

edge of the Acropolis. Here, nine months before the robe was to
be dedicated, and together with the Priestess of Athene, they set
up their loom. Although the subject matter was identical each year
(the conflict of the gods and giants) the precise design was chosen
annually by competition, an evolving pattern, ever changing and
yet essentially always the same.[28]

There on the Acropolis generations of young girls walked to and
fro in front of their great loom, secluded behind high walls from the
dust and din of all the building work.They were joined out on the
rock itself by other girls, marble girls, votive statues set up by the
richest families of Athens, pouting maidens with alluring eyes, their
long hair braided and cascading over girlish breasts, their bodies
draped in dresses painted with intoxicating geometric patterns,
hanging down in graceful folds to elegantly sandalled feet. Beside
them, statues of heroic and idealized young men sprang up with
smiling lips, some on horseback, others carrying young bullocks as
an offering to the city's patron goddess; and with them those most
aristocratic of all domesticated beasts: proud stallions and lean,
swift hunting dogs.

To be part of the life of the Acropolis was to be part of the elite.
Which was why Hipparchus' insult was so stinging. Hipparchus,
brother of the tyrant Hippias, had fallen in love with a young man,
Harmodius. But his advances were spurned. Harmodius already
had a lover, Aristogeiton. So Hipparchus plotted his revenge.
According to Thucydides,

> together with Hippias he invited one of Harmodius'
> sisters to become an Arrephoros, but when she
> presented herself, he sent her away, saying that she
> had never been chosen at all, and that she was not
> worthy of the post. Harmodius was greatly upset
> by this, and Aristogeiton, too, was infuriated on his

> behalf ... So they waited for the festival of the
> Great Panathenaia, which was the only day on
> which Athenians (taking part in the procession)
> could come together under arms without
> exciting suspicion.[29]

And so it was, at the Great Panathenaia of 514 BC, a
festival reconstituted by Peisistratus as part of an attempt to
strengthen Athens and enhance his city's feeling of identity,
that the enemies of Peisistratus' sons, members of great
rival families and disgruntled dynasties, mingled with the
celebrating throngs, their hearts set on murder. Who was the
true target, whether Hipparchus alone, or his brother, too, is
far from clear, for in the end hot heads and suspicious minds
meant that nothing went to plan:

> Harmodius and Aristogeiton had already drawn
> their daggers and were about to strike when they
> saw one of their cell in relaxed conversation
> with Hippias – not that Hippias was ever
> unapproachable. They jumped to the conclusion
> that the plot had been revealed and that they were
> about to be arrested. So they panicked ...

Dodging the crowds, they ran towards the city, and there
they saw Hipparchus and they took their chance. A sudden
knife blade flashing in the morning sun, and Hipparchus was
down. Confusion. Aristogeiton got away. Harmodius did not.
He was set upon by bodyguards and butchered.

The news spread quickly through the streets. Hippias,
not knowing if the violence was over or whether there were
more assassins hidden in the crowd, called for calm and

Opposite A marble maiden with almond eyes: one of the votive statues
set up on the Acropolis in the 6th century BC. Attica, Greece.

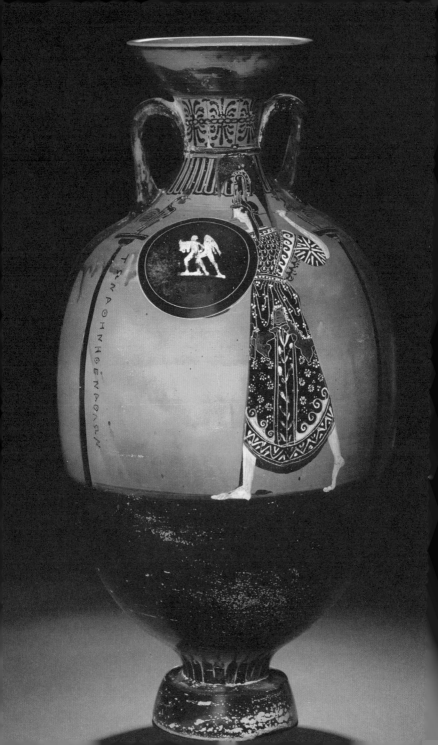

order. Quickly, he commanded everyone to lay down their spears and shields. Then he picked out those whom he suspected of involvement in the plot and had them searched. Any who were found to be concealing daggers were arrested and led off. Like Aristogeiton, when he was caught, they would not enjoy an easy death.

In a moment, an age of enlightenment was ended. From now on, increasingly paranoid, Hippias would rule Athens with an iron fist. As the sun sank behind Mount Aegaleus on that grim August night, silhouetting the Acropolis in a blaze of dying light, staining the writhing sculptures on the temple pediments blood red, there must have been many in the city who wondered with foreboding just what the future had in store.

Opposite Harmodius and Aristogeiton take pride of place on the shield of the beautifully attired Athene Promachos. Panathenaic amphora. Attica, Greece, 425–400 BC. H. 73.6 cm.

Chapter 2

Ground Zero

… the warlike deeds by which we acquired
our power, and the battles in which we and
our fathers gallantly resisted our enemies.[30]

On that hot August evening in 514 BC after the brutal butchering of
his brother Hipparchus, Hippias perhaps sought solace among the
shrines of the Athenian Acropolis. But just thirty-four years later
when his compatriots climbed the steep path to the plateau on a
grey September dawn in 480 BC, it must have seemed that they were
entering the world of nightmare. Where once temples had glittered
proudly in the rising sun, now there was nothing but an eerie, silent
landscape, dust and ash and charcoaled buildings, twisted corpses
and an acrid, drifting stench of smoke. All Hippias, Hipparchus and
Peisistratus, their father, had once sought to build was gone, and
the man who had helped to engineer this total, wanton, merciless
destruction had been Hippias himself.

Harmodius and Aristogeiton, assassins of Hipparchus, were not the
only men to harbour hatred for the family of Peisistratus. Almost forty
years after they had been driven into exile on a charge of sacrilege (see
p. 34), the Alcmaeonidae, granted amnesty at last, had returned to play
the game of politics from their estates in Attica (594 BC), and (perhaps)
to demonstrate their piety by helping fund the building of the limestone
temple of Athene on the Acropolis. But in the years of Peisistratus'

Opposite Persians bearing gifts: an infantryman in procession on a carved
limestone relief from Persepolis, in the Persian Empire, 358–338 BC. H. 75 cm.

ascendancy, some members of the family had once more been forced to leave the country (546 BC). Expatriates in foreign lands, they had plotted their rivals' downfall. And to achieve it, they had enlisted the power of the gods.

Nestling in a fold of wooded mountains above a fertile plain, Delphi was one of the most sacred places in the whole of Greece. Its oracle, by now the object of both pilgrimage and political patronage, had already proved influential in the affairs of Athens (see p. 30); and the shrewd Alcmaeonidae were quick to realize the potential benefits of encouraging its priests and wardens to support their cause. How they must have thanked the gods when, in 548 BC, a fire swept through the temple of Apollo, destroying it utterly and presenting the Alcmaeonidae with precisely the opportunity they had been looking for. In the words of Herodotus,

> they won the contract from the Delphic authorities to
> construct the temple which stands to this day ... They
> were a wealthy family, with a long and distinguished
> pedigree, and, in many ways, the temple which they
> built was superior to the specifications required,
> especially with regard to the facade. Here they used
> Parian marble, whereas the contract had been simply
> to use tufa throughout.[31]

So, as Peisistratus and his family were raising their temples and their shrines in Athens, in part to help confirm their supremacy there, at Delphi their enemies, the Alcmaeonidae, were adorning what was in effect an international Greek temple to Apollo, in the hope not only of further overturning their reputation for impiety but of underlining their status as one of the most powerful families in Greece. In the hope, too, of helping to secure the overthrow of the Peisistratids. Herodotus continues:

According to the Athenians, the Alcmaeonidae, while resident at Delphi, bribed the Priestess to let it be known to any Spartan who came to consult the oracle either on public business or privately, that it was Sparta's obligation to liberate Athens. The consequence of this continual repetition was that the Spartans sent ... an army to drive out the family of Peisistratus. They were on terms of friendship with them, but it made no difference. The gods' commands outweighed human allegiances.[32]

Above The ruins of the temple of Apollo at Delphi can be seen just beyond the theatre as day breaks over the shrine.

The Spartan intervention came in 510 BC. A first attack from the sea was beaten off by Hippias and his supporters, augmented by a squadron of 1000 cavalry from Thessaly. But shortly after, the Spartan king Cleomenes launched a land invasion into Attica at the head of a huge force. The Thessalians were routed, and more and more of Hippias' enemies flocked to the side of the liberators. As for Hippias himself and his supporters, they did what generations of embattled tyrants had done before them: they took refuge on the Acropolis. An attempt to smuggle Hippias' children out of Attica failed. They were arrested and held hostage. Hippias accepted terms. He would leave the country within five days.

With much of Greece now barred to them, Hippias packed into crates such treasures as he could and set off with his family east. In time, reports would trickle back to Athens of how Hippias had come first to the Bosphorus, to the court of his son-in-law, the tyrant of Lampsacus, and then, thanks to his influence, had disappeared deep into the mountain tracts of Asia on a journey of countless days and weeks, 1,800 miles (almost 3000 km) to Susa and the court of Darius, the Persian Great King.

Not that they had much time to think of Hippias in Athens. Or of Darius either. No sooner were the Alcmaeonidae removing the dust sheets from their ancestral mansions (and cancelling all work on Hippias' self-aggrandising temple of Olympian Zeus) than the Spartans were back at the Attic border. Things had not turned out quite as they had envisaged. The Alcmaeonidae, and especially one of their number, Cleisthenes, had been wasting no time in dismantling the trappings of tyranny (which, to the Spartans, were eminently acceptable) and replacing them with something which appeared on the surface at least to be a new, wide-ranging democracy (which, to the Spartans, was profoundly unacceptable).[33] Among Cleisthenes' many constitutional reforms, he organized the People into ten tribes, giving *gravitas* to each by naming them after a legendary Athenian hero, and making sure that all contained an element of each of the three factions which had once (in the days of Solon) threatened to tear the very fabric of society apart.

Yet even in Athens there were those who resisted change. Once again the old charge of impiety was dredged up by the Alcmaeonids' enemies. Once again the family was forced into exile. But when a pro-Spartan quisling tried to abolish the democratic Council, he found he had gone too far. The quisling and his Spartan backers (among them King Cleomenes) took refuge behind the gates of the Acropolis. Only the Priestess of Athene tried to resist them. She had been sitting in the temple porch, dozing on her chair by the door, when she was awakened by the clatter of running feet. She leapt up in alarm and, pointing at Cleomenes, she shouted: 'Go back, Spartan stranger! Do not enter this sacred place. No Spartan is allowed here!'[34]

Three days later, the two sides came to terms. The Spartans departed; the Alcmaeonidae returned. But although it was a minor episode and peace was soon restored, the consequences of this Spartan intervention would be felt long afterwards, and would lead, in part, not only to the burning of the temples on the Athenian Acropolis but to the building of the Parthenon itself.

For in these uncertain times, it was deemed sensible to attract support not only from the gods (as the Alcmaeonidae had done at Delphi) but from powerful neighbours, too. And the most powerful of them all, if also the most distant, was Persia. Even to acquire a pledge of support from Persia might be enough to deter a future attack from Sparta, and so it was that a small group of envoys set out not for the Persian capital Susa, many months away, but for one of its regional administrative centres, Sardis, so much closer, whose erstwhile king Croesus had once helped Greeks at Ephesus to build their temple to the goddess Artemis.

But in the years after that temple had been finished, great shifts had taken place in the politics of the east. Croesus had been too trusting of the close relationship with the divine which he believed his gifts to Artemis and her brother Apollo had bought him. According to Herodotus, he had been overly optimistic in his interpretation of an oracle from Delphi, which had advised him that, were he to attack the Persians, he would destroy a mighty empire. The empire he destroyed was his own. Into Croesus' territories exploded the mushrooming might of Persia, whose power had blossomed in less than fifty years so that it now controlled most of the Near and Middle East from the eastern Mediterranean to what is now Afghanistan and Uzbekistan, including Egypt and the southern shores of the Black Sea.

Now, charged with protecting the security of their new democracy, the Athenian envoys arrived in Sardis (507 BC). Perhaps the opulence they found bewildered them. Certainly the way the envoys handled their petition was nothing short of baffling.

> When they arrived and delivered their message, the governor asked them who these Athenians were, who sought to make an alliance with Persia, and where they lived. When they told him, he summarised the Persian position by explaining that Darius would make a treaty with them if they demonstrated their compliance by making the usual offerings of earth and water; if not, they must return home. Impatient to ratify the treaty, the envoys (acting on their own initiative) accepted the terms.[35]

What were they thinking of? Surely they cannot have begun to understand the consequences of their actions, for the offering of earth and water was the means by which conquered nations traditionally surrendered to the Persians. By willingly agreeing to these terms, the envoys were effectively relinquishing the sovereignty of Athens and declaring their land a vassal of the Persian Empire. As part of the deal, the Persians could now impose on the Athenians whatever governor they might see fit. And, from their point of view at least, the governor they chose had all the right credentials: not only had he proved his loyalty to Persia, he had the requisite experience as well. His father had been a powerful dynast. He himself had ruled for seventeen years. He was Athenian. He was Hippias.

Back in Athens, news of the treaty was greeted with disbelief. The People refused to ratify it. But it was no use. As far as the Persians were concerned, the terms were binding. If Athens did not willingly accept them, they would be imposed by force. Then, at this crucial moment, events intervened which would drag not only Athens but the whole of the eastern Greek world into total war.

Stretched like a necklace down the western coast of what is now Turkey, jewelled cities like Ephesus and Miletus, colonized centuries before by mainland Greeks, had already been sucked into the voracious maw of the Persian Empire. Not that they had put up much resistance. Irksome it may have been to pay tribute to the lackeys of the Great King, but, for the tyrants and aristocrats who could afford them, the luxuries that flowed back to their cities more than compensated. A contemporary poet and philosopher, Xenophanes, described how

> you can see them in their agoras, showing off
> their costly purple cloaks, drenched in intoxicating
> perfumes, tossing their expensively coiffed hair.[36]

To Athenian aristocrats looking east, these men of Ionia were the epitome of all that they themselves strove to be: wealthy, leisured and possessed of an orientalizing good taste embracing all the finer things of life. (Can this have been why those aristocratic Athenian envoys had agreed so willingly to offer Darius their gift of earth and water?) It was when the Ionians began to look west to democratic Athens that the trouble began.

Aristagoras, the tyrant of Miletus, felt under threat. He had inherited his rule from his uncle, Histiaeus, a man of immense energy and ambition, who had first proved his loyalty to Darius when serving with the Great King on campaign north of the Black Sea. Here he had opposed a proposal by a colleague, an Athenian called Miltiades, to destroy crucial bridges and so strand the Persians in the icy wastes. But then Histiaeus found himself detained indefinitely in Susa because he had demanded too ambitious a reward. Now, with his uncle's example before him, Aristagoras, too, was playing a high stakes game.

Above The temple of Artemis at Sardis, a successor to Cybele's temple, accidentally burned by the Athenians in 498 BC.

Caught between the citizens of Miletus lobbying for greater rights and his Persian overlords demanding proofs of loyalty, Aristagoras sought to shift the focus by persuading the Persians to launch an attack on the rich Greek island of Naxos. It was an unmitigated disaster. Aristagoras was held responsible. It was only a matter of time before he would be stripped of his tyranny. And worse. So he did what in the circumstances seemed the only thing to do. He threw in his lot with his fellow citizens, declared Miletus a democracy and so began a chain reaction which rattled the length and breadth of Ionia (499 BC).

War was inevitable. Hurriedly Aristagoras went on a diplomatic mission to the Greek mainland to enlist support. At Sparta he was rebuffed. At Athens, however, where its citizens were still trying desperately to pretend that they had not signed up to be a subject state of Persia, Aristagoras was welcomed with open arms. Soon an Athenian fleet of twenty warships, together with another five from the Euboean city of Eretria, was sailing east for Ionia.

While Aristagoras found reasons to remain in the comparative safety of Miletus, the combined force made for Sardis (498 BC). The Persian garrison was completely unprepared, and as Greek soldiers poured into the city, only those who could barricade themselves within the city's high acropolis were saved. Herodotus records what happened next:

> One of the houses was set alight by a soldier, and the fire spread quickly until all Sardis was burning. Even the suburbs were ablaze, and the native Lydian inhabitants, together with such Persians as were in the city, trapped in a ring of fire and unable to escape, ran into the agora, and there they made a stand ... In the fire which swept through Sardis, a temple of Cybele was burnt down, which the Persians subsequently used as an excuse to torch the temples in Greece.[37]

As Herodotus suggests, the burning of the temple in far-off Sardis would spark a conflagration which would, in time, engulf even the Acropolis in Athens. For now, though, the destruction of Sardis served to fan the flames of the Ionian Revolt. As the Athenian and Eretrian ships sailed back to Greece, job done, they left in their wake a seething cauldron of dissent, as city after city declared for freedom and democracy. It was not a situation that the Great King Darius could possibly allow.

For a few nail-biting years many of the rebel cities held off the Persian juggernaut, but by 494 BC, only Miletus was still free. For a while, the city with its three great harbours, jutting out into the turquoise sea on a long low narrow promontory, was protected by the combined fleet of Ionia, but when at last their ships engaged the Persians off the little island of Lade, morale disintegrated. Many of the 'allies' fled for home. Miletus was left open and exposed. It did not survive for long.

Herodotus catalogues the grim realities of their defeat:

> Most of the men were slaughtered by the Persians; the women and children were enslaved; and the temple at [nearby] Didyma, both the shrine and the oracle, was looted and burnt.[38]

Greeks considered temples to be inviolable. They did not burn them. Except by accident. For them, this deliberate torching of one of Ionia's most sacred shrines was an entirely new phenomenon of war. It broke the unwritten rules of engagement, which characterized conflict between 'civilized' peoples. It smacked of absolute barbarity.

When the news of Miletus' fall, and with it the end of the Ionian dream of freedom, crossed the sea to Athens, it plunged the city into deep despair. At the Festival of Dionysus early the next year, a leading playwright, Phrynichus produced a tragedy called *The Capture of Miletus*. The audience (all men of military age and over)[39] wept uncontrollably, for Athens had been Miletus' mother city. They banned the play from ever being performed again and fined Phrynichus the eye-watering sum of 1000 drachmas 'for reminding them of their own troubles'.[40]

Not that they needed much reminding. For years, stories had been circulating throughout Athens of how Darius had greeted the news of their involvement in the attack on Sardis:

> He demanded to know who these Athenians were, and,
> when he had found out, he asked to be given his bow.
> He took it, placed an arrow against the string and fired
> high into the air, with the words: 'God, grant that I might
> punish the Athenians!' And he ordered one of his servants
> to repeat to him three times, whenever he sat down to eat,
> the words: 'Master, remember the Athenians'.[41]

With Ionia now crushed, it did not require much imagination to work out which city would next feel the Persian Great King's wrath. If, sixty years before, Peisistratus had wanted to establish Athens as a major player on the stage of Greece, his descendants were now witnessing his wish come true. But not quite in the way he had intended.

A year after they had wept at Phrynichus' play, news reached the Athenians that the Persians were on the move. Under the command of the brilliant young general Mardonius, a great fleet and army had been mobilized. Their ultimate objective: Athens and Eretria. With mainland cities already falling to the advancing army and the north Aegean island of Thasos to the navy, it seemed but a matter of time before the Persians were marching south to Attica. But the weather intervened. Or perhaps it was the gods. As the Persian fleet was rounding the promontory of Athos, a gale blew up. Reports

claimed that 300 of their ships were lost and 20,000 men, smashed
in the racing foam against the slippery rocks. The expedition had
been brought to a sudden and disastrous conclusion. Athens and her
temples had been saved.

But not for long. If anyone believed that this was the end of
the Persian threat, they would soon find themselves mistaken. A
year later, news came to the Athenians of parties of Persian envoys
touring mainland Greece, demanding earth and water, offering
good terms to any city that would join their empire. Worryingly for
Athens, the islanders of Aegina, clearly visible from the Acropolis,
had accepted the Persians' terms. The enemy was quite literally on
their doorstep. The envoys soon turned up in Athens, too. How they
approached the question of earth and water is not recorded. How
they were received, however, is. The Athenians threw them into a
deep pit and left them there to die. They had asked for Athenian
earth; now they had got it. In Sparta, in a suspiciously neat parallel,
another group of envoys was dropped into a well.

Once more, the gauntlet had been thrown down; once more
Darius responded. In 490 BC, a Persian fleet was sailing west from
Ionia, its prows slicing a path directly towards its twin goals: the
island of Euboea, home to Eretria, and the coast of Attica. On
its way it settled an old score. Aristagoras' unsuccessful attempt to
capture Naxos had contributed to the Ionian Revolt; this time defeat
was not an option. When the islanders saw the Persian fleet, 600
strong, bearing down on their harbour, they fled to the hills. Those
who were found were sold into slavery. As for their city, the Persians
put it to the torch. Nothing was spared, not even the temples. Which
made the Persians' next move all the more ominous. For, from
Naxos they set course north towards the most sacred island of them
all: Delos.

Legend told how, fleeing from the wrath of Hera, with whose
husband Zeus' children she was pregnant, the goddess Leto had

finally arrived at Delos. Here, among the quails which haunt the tiny scrubby island, she had given birth to those two radiant divinities, Apollo and Artemis. The palm tree to which, in labour, she was said to have clung was revered in historical times, and rich temples and treasuries were built on the flat land by the shallow harbour and on the slopes of the low hill. Indeed, Peisistratus himself had added to the island's sanctity, relocating ancient tombs from near the temples to another part of Delos, in response, so he claimed, to an oracle.[42]

With Naxos' temples now destroyed and blanketed in ash, no one can have held much hope for Delos. And yet, the site was spared. The only smoke to belly into the crystal summer sky came from 300 talents' weight of frankincense (17,100 lbs, 9,660 kg), burnt on the ancient altar by its new Persian overlords, a fragrant offering. That Delos was spared may have been thanks to the presence of one man, elderly now, but no less determined to regain what he still saw as his birthright. For standing by the altar on that August day was Hippias, son of Peisistratus, who had so honoured Delos. In a matter of weeks, or so he hoped, Hippias would be back in Athens where he belonged, ruling once more as tyrant.

First, though, Euboea and Eretria. Watching from their walls as, with grim efficiency, Persian horses were led off ships and infantrymen swarmed in their tens of thousands on to the crowded beach, Eretria's inhabitants were panic stricken. Within hours, the assault began. Six days it lasted. In the end the city was betrayed by two of its own leading men. As the population was led off in chains to slavery,[43] the temples were despoiled of all their offerings. And then the fires were lit.

With black smoke belching from the temples of Eretria, the Persians sailed across the narrow strait to mainland Greece, where on the sloping beach they dragged their ships out of the sea at Marathon. After twenty years, Hippias was home in Attica. While his supporters still in Athens secretly rejoiced, to his enemies, members of rival dynasties and devotees of democracy, the seemingly inexorable approach of the Persians heralded not only the destruction of all they had striven so hard to build, but their own death and the enslavement of their families. It was not something they would accept without a fight.

Already envoys had been sent to most of the Greek city states to urge them to send troops to help to fight the Persians. The Spartans expressed their willingness – but, for religious reasons, they could not set out before the full moon, and that was more than a week away. Only the tiny city of Plataea west of Attica had sent 1000 men. And now, with the 10,000 or so hoplite foot soldiers of Athens, they had marched out from the city, skirting Mount Pentelicon, to Marathon, where they had taken their position on high ground sacred to the hero Heracles. These hoplites were the yeoman land-owners of Attica, who even in the new democracy held special rights of membership of Athens' legislative council, and whose status empowered them to don their armour, and to interlock their heavy shields of wood and metal, round and bevelled, a metre in diameter, and fight in the phalanx for their country.

But never to be generals. That rank was reserved for the ancient aristocracy, the richest moneyed families of them all. Yet in the field even these supreme commanders were constrained by a democratic egalitarianism, as ultimate authority rotated on a daily basis between each of the ten generals. At least in theory. In fact, many of them realized how such a system could potentially cause chaos, so, bowing to his experience, they agreed to relinquish their command to their colleague, Miltiades.

Miltiades it was who, years before, had tried to strand Darius and his army in the ice-fields north of the Black Sea (see p. 56). The latest of a family of wealthy Athenians who had ruled the Gallipoli Peninsula as tyrants, he had found his lands first threatened and then annexed by the Persians. At first he had professed allegiance to his new masters (even

while plotting their destruction), but come the Ionian Revolt he had thrown his weight behind the rebels. When Miletus fell, he had fled to Athens, where rival patricians had soon (if grudgingly) welcomed him into the fold. Miltiades, after all, had first-hand knowledge of Persian tactics, and now he would put it to the test.

Precisely what happened at Marathon on that September morning (490 BC) is lost in the afterglow of propaganda and myth-making. To the Greek hoplites, heavily outnumbered, it was nothing short of miraculous. So many days of anxious waiting; so many days of impotently watching the Persians on the shoreline from their

Above Model chariot in gold from the Oxus Treasure (east Persian Empire). Achaemenid, 5th–4th century BC. H. 7.5 cm; L. 19.5 cm.

vantage point beside the shrine of Heracles; and then at dawn, as
the sun rose hot above the mountains of Euboea, at last the order
came. It may be that in the hours before, in the glow of the full
moon, the scouts had seen the Persian horses being embarked on
to the ships. It may be that Miltiades had realized just what this
embarkation meant: that the Persians were going to put to sea and
sail around Cape Sounion, with its limestone temple to Poseidon
rising proudly on its headland, to Athens, now denuded of its men
and tender for the taking. Whatever his reason and whatever the
odds, when the generals made sacrifice, they found the omens
favourable. The gods were on their side.

The order given, the hoplites advanced in tight formation. A mile
they had to cover, north towards the vast encampment of the enemy.
As they came ever closer, and the dark hail of Persian arrows began
to thump and rattle on their shields and sink into the earth around
them, the Greeks, counter to all training they had ever had, counter,
too, to any rationale of hoplite warfare, broke into a run, smashing
an unstoppable scythe of crashing bronze, an inexorable bristling
of spears, into the Persian infantry. Only the crack troops of the
Persian centre held firm, and in time even they were defeated. As for
the rest, poorly equipped, perhaps less loyal, they turned and fled,
some to the reedy marshland to their rear, where they were trapped
and butchered, others to the ships. With the Greeks pursuing the
fugitives into the surf, trying desperately to prevent them from
escaping, the Persian fleet scrambled to put out to sea, leaving any
who had not embarked to their inevitable fate. For the Greeks,
the battle had been won. And yet, they could not celebrate. They
had seen where the Persian ships were heading. South. Towards
Sounion. Their intentions were all too clear. The Persians may
have lost the battle, but their real goal remained Athens. And with
Athens' army still at Marathon, the city lay wide open.

Leaving a detachment to mop up at Marathon (and guard the

stockpiles of eastern treasure which had been abandoned on the battlefield), Miltiades led the rest of his desperately tired army on a grim march back across the foothills of Pentelicon, an urgent race to reach the city and its ports before the Persians. From the Attic shore, they saw the Persian fleet lying lazily at anchor off the bay at Phaleron. Then, miraculously, it was gone, sails hoisted, scudding back across the empty sea to Asia.

The threat was lifted. Single-handed (give or take the 1000 hoplites from Plataea), Athens had stood fast against the might of Persia. And won. When the Spartans did arrive in Athens, two days too late, the Athenians took pleasure in escorting them to Marathon and showing off the corpses of the dead. According to their calculations they had killed 6,400 Persians. On their own side they had lost 192 men, on whom they bestowed the honour of being buried side by side beneath a great mound on the battlefield where they had fallen. At a time when Athens and her new democracy had found itself under threat, these men had been among the first to fall protecting it. Even Athens' ancient heroes had stood resolutely by them, for

> many of those who had fought at Marathon believed that they had seen the phantom form of Theseus, full-armoured, charge in front of them against the Persian ranks.[44]

In time, those who had fallen at Marathon themselves took on heroic status. Like those noble characters from Athenian mythology, King Codrus or the daughters of Erechtheus, and like the tyrant-slayers Aristogeiton and Harmodius, the city's hoplites had laid down their lives for Athens. And not just for Athens. For all of Greece as well.

In Athens itself, the mood of celebration was enhanced by news of Hippias' death at Lemnos on his voyage back to Persia, but still there was political infighting. Rumours swirled through the city streets that members of the Alcmaeonidae had been observed at Marathon, flashing signals to the Persians – rumours which, although untrue, showed nonetheless how torn by faction Athens still remained.

And yet the city pulled together. At Delphi, below the Alcmaeonidae's great gleaming temple, the Athenian democracy set up a treasury in which to store and show off some of the booty they had plundered from the Persians – a building which was both a dedication to Apollo and a beacon to the world of Athens' role in saving Greece. In Athens, too, on the Acropolis they celebrated Marathon. A slender column was erected, bearing a statue of winged Victory, a memorial to a general who had fallen on the battlefield. Engraved on it were words linking Victory, 'the herald of the gods who live in the palaces of Mount Olympus', with the Athenians who 'fought at Marathon in defence of Greece'. Already Marathon was entering the world of myth.

Unsurprising then that the People decided to demolish the ancient limestone temple of Athene at the south of the Acropolis and to build in its place a new temple, an offering of thanks for victory at Marathon, paid for not by a self-publicising plutocrat but by the Athenian People from the spoils of war. So, while for now the temple to Athene Polias, home to olive *xoanon*, was allowed to remain intact, from its sister temple the archaic sculptures were removed, the limestone blocks dismantled, the old columns taken down, while the platform on which the building had once rested was enlarged to house its new democratic successor. And so, the backcloth to the years that followed: the hewing of marble; its transportation from the quarries in through the city and up the ramp to the Acropolis; the shaping of new columns; their positioning; their growth; a new silhouette emerging on the sacred rock, the promise of a temple which would never, in the end, be completed.

Opposite A Persian's face is frozen in fear while (above) one of his compatriots serves a Greek woman as her slave. Drinking mug, Attica, Greece, 410–400 BC. H. 23.5 cm.

E 791

For the optimism after Marathon was premature. Athens' ruling families may have been united against a common enemy but, with that enemy gone, factionalism was never far away. One of its first victims was Miltiades, the victor of Marathon himself. In a fit of profiteering zeal, he led an expedition against Paros, promising to bring home untold wealth. It ended in disaster. Returning on a stretcher with a wounded knee (now gangrenous), Miltiades found himself in court on the capital charge of defrauding the People. And acting on the People's behalf, no doubt professing breathtaking public spiritedness, appeared a ruthlessly ambitious prosecutor, Xanthippus, a leading member of the Alcmaeonidae. Miltiades was condemned. But not executed. Instead of the death penalty he was fined fifty talents, enough to bankrupt him.[45] And when Miltiades died of his wounds a short time later (489 BC), the fine was inherited by his son, the tall, dark, mop-headed womaniser Cimon. To the Alcmaeonidae, it must have seemed as if one rival family had been neutralized.

Yet there were times in these frantic years when even opposing dynasts could agree. In the hills just north of Sounion a rich vein of silver was found at Laurium (483 BC). Apart from the money made by affluent investors, the workings were profiting the public coffers too. To curry favour with the voters, populist politicians urged that these profits be divided equally among the People, but one man resisted this appeal.

Bull necked and bull headed, Themistocles was a member of the ruling elite. He had fought at Marathon; he may even have been one of the ten generals. From an early age he had sought to woo the People, while emulating the best families in his support of the arts, sponsoring plays by Phrynichus and letting musicians practise in his house.[46] Now (482 BC) in the Assembly he took his stand to advocate a policy that would deprive the People of the very windfall which others were urging they should have. Instead of universal handouts, he argued, the revenue from Laurium should be used to build a fleet: 100 triremes, war ships with which the People could enhance their power and defeat the island of Aegina, which so recently had given earth and water to the Persians and now was threatening Athens' trade. Not to mention that 100 ships would need 20,000 oarsmen, drawn from the poorest classes of Athenian society, and guaranteeing them a constant source of income.[47] On a show of hands, his proposal scraped through.

Hindsight would suggest that the cunning Themistocles had another and more subtle reason for proposing the construction of his 100 ships. Across the Aegean, the boatyards of the Persians, too, were resounding to the rasp of saws and the rhythm of hammers, and the beaches were boiling with the reek of hot tar slapped on fresh-planed keels. Four years before, in 486 BC, Darius, scourge of Ionia, Naxos and Euboea, had died. Now his son, the volatile, dangerous, sardonic Xerxes had ascended to the Persian throne, and he meant to finish what Darius had begun. Tortured by the memory of Marathon, he was intent on vengeance. And there were many in his court who sought to keep his anger simmering. Not least the family of Hippias, still harbouring ambitions to rule Athens.[48]

For months the air on both sides of the Aegean broiled with rumour and expectancy. When news came that Persian troops were massing at Sardis, where less than a generation earlier Athenians had accidentally burned the temple of Cybele, Greek spies were sent to try to assess their numbers. The spies were captured, but Xerxes ordered that their lives be spared. Instead he sent them on a tour of his whole army, and home to Greece with paralysing news. The Persian force was so large it defied all computation.[49] And it was drawn from every territory within Xerxes' sprawling empire. Trousered Persians with fish-mail tunics and large wicker shields marched side by side with Ethiopians in leopard skins, their spearheads fashioned from the bones of antelopes; a regiment from India marched with other, eastern Ethiopians, whose headdresses were fashioned out of horses' scalps, the ears erect, the manes flowing as a helmet crest; still others rode on horseback or in chariots drawn by horses or wild asses, while, towering over all of them, camel riders from Arabia brought up the rear. And at the army's heart were the Ten Thousand, a corps of hand-picked fighters, nicknamed 'The Immortals', because if any of their number should be killed or injured, his place would immediately be filled by a reserve.

As Xerxes had foreseen, the spies' reports sowed panic. When Persian envoys next toured Greece (pointedly by passing both Athens and Sparta, where their hapless colleagues had been so summarily despatched a decade earlier), many cities did not hesitate before making offerings of earth and water. Meanwhile Xerxes, in an extravagance of showmanship, was demonstrating to any waverers that it was in his power not only to take Greek water and Greek earth but to transform them into their opposites. Having paused at Troy, where he sacrificed 1000 oxen and poured libations, vowing to avenge its legendary destruction at the hands of Greeks, Xerxes oversaw the first of these miracles: the metamorphosis of water into dry land. Where the turbid currents of the Bosphorus debouch into the North Aegean, his engineers built a bridge of boats so that the army's crossing might be made as if on land. And through the promontory of Athos, where Mardonius' Persian fleet had foundered, he ordered a canal cut so that his navy sailed where once had been dry land. The symbolism was unmistakable. Nothing and no one could withstand the might of Xerxes. There was no point in even trying.

Many of the Greeks agreed. But by no means all. War councils had already formulated strategies, and this time most of the cities of the Peloponnese were determined to play their part. So not only Athens' hoplites, veterans of Marathon, but her newly created navy too (now swollen to 200 ships) joined a confederation of Greek states as diverse as affluent Corinth and tiny Plataea. And Sparta, they agreed, should lead them.

As the Persians swung south towards them, the Greek

Opposite A trousered Persian, accompanied by his retinue, rides a Bactrian camel. Red-figure *lekythos* (for storing oil). Attica, Greece, 410–400 BC. H. 23.5 cm.

confederation acted (August 480 BC). To reach Attica, the enemy must negotiate a narrow pass between the mountains and the sea, where sulphur springs imbued the landscape with an eerie, otherworldly atmosphere and gave the place its name: Thermopylae (The Hot Gates). Here, while their allies massed near Corinth, a small band of Spartans headed north to stage a holding operation, while the Greek fleet sailed round Cape Sounion to Euboea's northernmost tip, there to await the coming of the Persians.

In Athens, nerves were stretched to breaking point. Opinion was divided between those who advocated abandoning the city and those who urged staying to fight, protected inside the walls of the Acropolis. So envoys had been sent to Delphi to consult the oracle. Its first response had been disastrous. Choked with images of death, it urged them to

> leave your homes and the Acropolis, which your city
>   circles like a wheel …
> All is destroyed. Fire and Ares, rushing god of war,
> Who bears down on you in his Syrian chariot, will
>   lay you low.
> He will … consume in flames so many shrines of gods,
> Which stand now, oozing sweat and trembling with fear,
> While over rooftops black blood surges.[50]

It was not what the Athenians wanted to hear. So, in an unprecedented act of perseverance, the envoys put their question once again. This time, the response was slightly better:

> Athene cannot completely win over the heart of
>   Olympian Zeus
> Though she begs him incessantly with many prayers
>   and all her guile …

Although all of the rest of Attica is captured …

Nonetheless, Zeus, the all-seeing, grants to Athene
   her plea

That the wooden wall alone shall not be taken, but will
   protect you and your children.

Do not wait for the great army of cavalry and infantry
   which comes from Asia.

Do not stay still. But turn and withdraw from the enemy.

In truth, the day will come when you will face him.

God-like Salamis, you will be the cause of death to
   women's sons

When the grain is scattered or the harvest gathered in.[51]

If the first response spelled inescapable disaster, the second held
out hope, however tenuous. But what did it mean? What was the
wooden wall which alone would not be taken? Traditionalists
argued that it was the wooden palisade which circled the Acropolis.
Surely the oracle meant them to stay and fight. But Themistocles'
supporters believed otherwise. To them the wooden wall denoted
something altogether different and (appropriately for the artful
Athene) much more cunning: it was the 200 ships of Athens' new
fleet built in the hurried months before. The gods were urging them
to abandon Athens and trust to the fleet.

   In Athens, as ever, debate was boundless. But then they heard the
news. The Spartans had been massacred at Thermopylae. The allied
fleet was heading home. The time for talking was over. It took a young
aristocrat to demonstrate the leadership which the situation so cried
out for. At the head of a crowd of friends and colleagues, Cimon, son
of the once-revered Miltiades, processed from the city gates

      up to the Acropolis. In his hands he carried his horse's
      bridle as an offering to Athene, to show that what Athens

needed in that hour was not cavalry, but men to fight at
sea. He dedicated the bridle, and, taking a shield which
was hanging in the temple, he offered prayers to Athene.
And then he walked down to the sea.[52]

At the same time, on the Acropolis, another prodigy had been
observed. The snake which the Athenians worshipped as the
embodiment of Erichthonius had disappeared. Its monthly offering
of honey cakes had been untouched. Athene had abandoned the
Acropolis. Why should her people stay?

So began the evacuation of Athens. Women, children and the
elderly, freeborn and foreigners and slaves, each clutching such
possessions as they could salvage, crowded the quayside at Piraeus,
from where, in an urgent race against time, they were ferried in a
flotilla of fishing boats and warships across the gulf to Troezen or
to Salamis. With them, lovingly wrapped in its sacred robe, went
the *xoanon*, the ancient statue of Athene, the embodiment of the
very soul of Athens.

On the Acropolis, with its temples, one to Athene Polias,
Protectress of the City, the other, half-finished, a monument
to Marathon, only a handful of people remained behind the
barricades: temple wardens, who felt their fate was inexorably
linked with that of the shrines they served; diehards, who refused
to abandon Athens to a newfangled citizens' navy; and members
of the very poor, who (by design or accident) had been left behind
when the boats had sailed. From where Peisistratus had once gazed
with brimming satisfaction on his burgeoning city, the last rump of
stalwarts watched over a silent ghost town and awaited the Persians.

They saw the smoke pall from burning villages and farmsteads
first, grey clouds drifting from the country shrines and temples.
Then, pouring in across the Attic plain, engulfing vineyards, fields
and olive groves, flowing past the pinnacle of Lycabettus, down to

the city walls and through the gates, the vast horde of the Persians themselves. Soon, they had occupied the Areopagus (where in mythology invading Amazons had once camped), the Hill of Ares, god of war, a mere sling-shot from the Acropolis. Soon, a storm of blazing arrows was buffeting the very walls in which they put their faith. Soon, Xerxes' men had found a way up onto the rock itself.

In the desolate words of Herodotus

> When they saw them on the Acropolis, some of the Athenians threw themselves from the wall to their death, while others sought sanctuary in the temple's innermost shrine. But the Persians flung open the doors and slaughtered everyone inside. They left no one alive. Then they looted the temple treasures and set fire to everything on the Acropolis.[53]

Temples and statues, memorials and shrines – all were reduced to rubble. How Hippias' children felt as they surveyed the scene can only be imagined. The city they had regarded as their birthright, the vision of Peisistratus their grandfather, had been destroyed by their Persian champions. Next day, as if to rub salt into their already gaping wounds, Xerxes commanded them to go up onto the Acropolis and make sacrifice 'following the traditions of Athens'.[54] How could they refuse?

The dust and ash they had expected, and the carnage, too. But as the collaborators picked their way through the rubble of their city's once proud past, skirting the still-smouldering ruins of the temple of Athene Polias, its ancient statue safe somewhere on Salamis, they came across the charcoaled stump of the sacred olive tree which Athene (it was said) herself had planted. And what they saw there chilled them to the bone.

Chapter 3

Imperial Revenge

Our adventurous spirit has forced an
entry into every sea and every land;
and everywhere we have left behind us
everlasting memorials of good done to
our friends or suffering inflicted on our
enemies.[55]

The sight which greeted the collaborators' eyes was nothing short
of a miracle, though for them it was an omen presaging disaster.
In the muffled silence of the still-smoking Acropolis, from the
scorched stump of the olive tree, seared by the heat of the previous
day's fire, there sprouted a green shoot. Already it was 18 inches
(46 cm) long.[56] The sign was clear. Athene had spoken. The city may
have been defeated, her temples and her shrines destroyed, but her
life-force still lived on. Athens would be reborn. Death would be
followed by rebirth.

To the loyal Athenians camped on the beaches of Salamis,
their triremes drawn up beyond the water's edge, the omen, had
they learned of it, would have been a welcome tonic. But perhaps
they were thinking anyway of the mysterious cycles of death and
rebirth. For in a few days (in more settled times) they would have
celebrated the Great Mysteries in the sanctuary so tantalizingly in
view across the bay at Eleusis. Still, the horror of the black smoke

Opposite Athene, wearing her snake-fringed *aegis*, brandishes a ship's 'ram' in
her left hand. Red-figure amphora. Attica, Greece, *c.* 470–450 BC. H. 34.3 cm.

belching from a blazing Athens into the early September skies, may have been mitigated slightly by the words of the oracle with its imagery of crops (so central to the Mysteries):

> God-like Salamis, you will be the cause of death to
>   women's sons
> When the grain is scattered or the harvest gathered in.

Especially if they, too, had seen another omen, reported by an Athenian exile in Xerxes' army:

> a cloud of dust, like a cloud raised by a marching
> army, 30,000 strong [i.e., the size of Athens' citizen
> population] coming from Eleusis … and the sound of
> voices [singing] the hymn, sung at the Mysteries …
> The dust-cloud rose into the sky and drifted across to
> Salamis, where the Greek fleet was stationed.[57]

Were the gods intervening? Were the pieces of the jigsaw falling into place? Here were the Greeks on Salamis. Now was the time when the cycles of the crops would normally be celebrated at the Mysteries. All that remained was to engineer the death of women's sons. But whose were these sons? Greeks or Persians? And if, as they hoped, it was the Persians, how were the Athenians to contrive the encounter which would cause the oracle to come true?

The conundrum was solved by Themistocles himself. He sent a Persian-speaking slave to Xerxes to inform him that the Greek fleet, frightened of being bottle-necked at Salamis, was planning that night to make a dash for Corinth. The bait was swallowed, the Persian fleet launched, and all night Xerxes' ships, their crews alert to any motion, patrolled the waters of the channel mouths. Only at dawn did the Greek oarsmen waken and, having offered sacrifices to

the gods for victory, take their seats on the rowing benches and
so put out to sea.

The battle was hard fought but in the end, just as at Marathon,
the determination and the discipline of the Greeks won through.
Snarled in unfamiliar waters, outmanoeuvred and outwitted,
watched by the merciless eyes of Xerxes from his golden throne
on Mount Aegaleus, his scribes poised to record a famous victory,

Above The gods of Eleusis, including Demeter and Persephone, are
shown before a pillared building. Red-figure bell-krater. Attica, Greece,
c.380–360 BC. H. 51.4 cm.

the Persian ships were rammed and routed. As their crews sought
to swim to safety they were speared 'like shoals of tuna fish'.[58]
Only one of his admirals excited Xerxes' praise. When he saw
the flagship of Artemisia, his client queen of Caria, bravely ram a
sluggish trireme, he exclaimed, 'My men have turned into women,
my women into men!'[59] Only later did Xerxes learn that the ship she
had attacked had been one of his own fleet, blocking her escape.

Once again, and thanks to an Athenian, the might of Persia had
been broken. Once again, a matter of days later, what remained
of the Persian fleet was scudding back across the sea to the ports
of Asia Minor. And, as they did so, Xerxes himself, at the head of
much of his vast army, marched out of Attica north and away across
what were by now the icy plains of Thessaly, and back across his
bridge of boats towards the scented gardens and the royal harems
of Susa. But he left in Greece his general Mardonius, now with a
leaner, tougher force of elite troops, and Persian gold with which to
bribe his way to victory. Defeated on both land and sea the Persians
may have been, but they were still determined to claim the earth
and water which they deemed was theirs by right, and it mattered
little how they achieved it.

As the Athenians returned to their devastated city,
unrecognizable amid the rubble of once familiar landmarks, and
settled into tents and huts to shelter as best they could against the
winter rains and snow, an envoy arrived from Mardonius. The
Persians were offering terms of almost unbelievable generosity.
Xerxes had sent a message to Mardonius:

> I am prepared to overlook all I have suffered at the hands of
> Athens. Restore their land to the Athenians, Mardonius, and
> in addition let them take any territory they wish and have
> self-government. If they agree to terms, you must in turn
> rebuild the temples which I burned.[60]

Such magnanimity! And yet, if they accepted, Athens would forever
be in Persia's debt. For the Athenians it was too high a price.
Already they had climbed the ramp onto the charred Acropolis
where they had gathered everything that they could find – from
chunks of sculpture blackened in the smoke to shattered bowls to
sixty silver coins, fused by the intense heat[61] – and buried them in
specially dug pits. Their feelings can only be imagined. Humiliation?

Above A fragment of a vase burned in Xerxes' torching of the Acropolis shows
Hermes and a well-groomed horse. Attica, Greece, c.490–480 BC. H. 45.5 cm.

Anger? Determination to get even with their enemy? Certainly capitulation was not on the agenda. Nor was disunity among the allies. As their response to Mardonius made clear, the Athenians well understood that to preserve their city's hard-won freedom they must preserve the freedom of all Greece:

> The whole world does not contain such wealth or such fine lands that we would accept them in payment to join Persia and to enslave Greece. So much forbids us, and not least the burning of the temples and the statues of our gods, now nothing but dust and debris. To avenge such violation, not to clasp the hands of those who did it, is our duty. It would be shameful to betray the Greeks, our people, united in one blood, one language, in our temples and our rituals, our common customs. So, know this: as long as there is one Athenian left on this earth alive, we shall never make peace with Xerxes.[62]

To Mardonius it must have seemed like so much bluster and bravado. With the spring he was marching south again, and the boats were once more ferrying its population out of Attica (479 BC). By June the Persian Immortals were once more in control of the Acropolis, and Marathon and Salamis seemed distant memories.

But once more too Greece rallied, and soon beneath the blistering August sun near the tiny city of Plataea, whose hoplites just eleven years before had fought at Marathon, the armies of the free Greek states locked shields to face the Persians. But before the fighting, it was subsequently said, they swore an oath whose implications would be felt on the Athenian Acropolis for thirty years. For according to later historians it included this clause:

> I shall not rebuild any of the temples or the shrines
> burned and demolished by the Persians, but shall let
> them remain in ruins, a reminder of the Persians'
> impiety for all generations still to come.[63]

With the Persians massing across the river at Plataea, the Greeks
needed no reminder of the stakes that they were playing for.
Outnumbered as they were, especially by the Persian cavalry, the
terrain did not favour a direct attack. Instead, they must wait. And
watch. And so they did for days on end, while the Persians cut off
first their food supplies and then their water. The Greeks were under
siege. They tried to execute an organised withdrawal. It turned
into a shambles. It was the moment that Mardonius was waiting
for. Ruthlessly, he mounted his white horse and, surrounded by his
Immortals, he gave the order to attack. For the Greeks, caught in
the confusion of retreat, the situation was desperate. With lines
of communication stretched or non-existent, there could be no
coordinated strategy. Armies from diverse states found themselves
cut off from central command. All they could hope was that
their bravery and resolution might be matched by those of allies
elsewhere on the field. It was. At last, as fighting swirled around
him, Mardonius himself was toppled from his horse and killed.
Deprived of their leader, his troops lost heart. They turned and fled,
streaming in their tens of thousands from the battlefield, running
panic stricken from the pursuing Greeks. It was a bloodbath.
According to Herodotus, as many as 250,000 Persians were killed for
the loss of just over 1000 Greeks.[64]

As the survivors scoured the plain, picking their way among
the corpses of the dead, they came across a wondrous pavilion, a
silken tent with many rooms, hung with the richest tapestries and
furnished with couches, beds and tables inlaid with ivory. It was
so fabulous they thought it must have been the tent of Xerxes, left

behind when the Great King fled to Persia. The height of luxury, it was a perfect metaphor for the tyranny and avarice the Greeks had been resisting. Yet paradoxically, within a few short decades, it would be replicated without any seeming irony in the very heart of Athens by a man who claimed to be the champion of democracy (see Chapter 6).

With the spoils divided and trophies set up to commemorate their victory, the Greeks dispersed home to their cities to savour Mardonius' defeat. Their celebrations were made all the sweeter by the news of a second victory. The very day they had been fighting at Plataea (or so it was conveniently claimed), across the Aegean in the shadow of Mount Mycale, where the free cities of Ionia had once met in congress, an army of Greek allies had engaged the rump of Xerxes' own retreating troops and, in a long and bloody battle, had defeated them.

The threat of Persian invasion had been lifted. But for how long? Recent history had shown that the Persians had not only the resources but the tenacity to launch attack after attack on Greece. Who was to say that they would not be back again within another ten years? Who was to say the Greeks could again withstand them? Swept forward on the wave of victory, surely the best course was to take the battle on to Persian soil.

So, as the citizens of Athens were clearing rubble from their streets and beginning the laborious process of rebuilding city walls and houses, out in the east one of their generals was spearheading the attacks against the Persians. Xanthippus, the Alcmaeonid who had so ruthlessly prosecuted Marathon's victor Miltiades ten years before, had led the Athenian forces to victory at Mycale. Now he sailed north to the Dardanelles, where he first commandeered as plunder the hawsers which had held together Xerxes' bridge of boats, and then captured the Persian stronghold of Sestus. His treatment of its commander sent shockwaves throughout Greece, for he took him

Above Young Ethiopians like this one played a major role in Xerxes' army.
Alabastron (used for holding oil). Attica, Greece, *c.*480 BC. H. 16 cm.

> to the headland where Xerxes' bridge had been …
> and nailed him to a plank and crucified him. His son
> was stoned to death as he looked on. Then the fleet set
> sail for Greece, weighed down with booty, including
> the cables of Xerxes' bridge, which the Athenians
> meant to dedicate as an offering in their temples.[65]

Perhaps, in their bloodlust, they had forgotten for a moment that the temples were all gone, and that their world had undergone a seismic change. Yet cracks had already appeared in the old order. Already old alliances were splintering.

Sparta, ever reluctant to campaign far from her borders, had proposed that the Ionians abandon their cities and relocate to mainland Greece – the only way, it argued, to ensure protection from the Persians. The Ionians met the suggestion with hostility. They refused to submit to Spartan leadership a moment longer and chose instead to place at their head an Athenian, a young man who had already proved his charismatic powers of leadership at home and on campaign: Cimon, whose dedication of his bridle on the Acropolis had so galvanized his comrades to take to the sea at Salamis. It was an ideal solution. The Spartans could stay close to home. The Ionians had as their leaders the Athenians, their cousins. The Athenians assumed what they considered their rightful role as leaders of Ionia. And as for Cimon, while the appointment may have brought him into closer conflict with his father's nemesis, Xanthippus and the Alcmaeonidae, it was the kind of conflict that both he and Athens thrived on.

For, although Athens trumpeted her democratic constitution, in fact the reins of power still rested firmly in the hands of wealthy families, as they had always done. True, important decisions were taken on Pnyx Hill in the Popular Assembly overlooking the now blackened Acropolis. But while in theory this was a committed gathering of all the citizens of Attica, in practice few of the country dwellers could afford the time to journey to the city, and many urban Athenians were less than enthusiastic about sacrificing valuable working hours to listen to interminable speeches.[66] And as for those speeches, by no means everyone was sufficiently educated or confident to stand up and address thousands of potentially hostile hecklers. In reality the Assembly was dominated by a few men, who had somehow won the citizens' respect – often successful generals, whose orders they obeyed while on campaign, and whose proposals they would ratify in the Assembly.

No one understood this better than Cimon. Tirelessly he worked to win his city's approval and achieve his dream of power. Victories on campaign had meant he had accrued great personal wealth. So now, like Peisistratus before him, he won approbation not just through his public generosity – he provided food and clothing to the city's poor and allowed free access to his estates in Attica (which were 'large enough to be those of a tyrant')[67] – but through his building works as well. Thanks (it was later explained) to the Oath of Plataea the ruined temples could not be rebuilt, but there were other possibilities and Cimon seized them in both hands. In the dusty Agora he planted shady plane trees, while, outside the city walls, he

> transformed the Academy [originally a copse sacred to the hero Academus] from an arid scrubby wasteland into a beautifully irrigated grove, which he enhanced with shady walkways and level race-tracks.[68]

A Persian visitor might have confused it with an imperial pleaure garden. In addition Cimon used his new wealth to drain and reclaim the land between the city and Piraeus, while from the fruits of his foreign wars, he rebuilt the southern bastion of the Acropolis, enlarging the plateau, and enhancing its appearance of

impregnability. Yet, frustratingly, on the Acropolis itself, there was
little he could do. The Oath of Plataea had seen to that.

True, some work was carried out: sacrifices, after all, still had to be
offered at the altars, and perhaps a makeshift shed had been erected
to accommodate the ancient olive-wood statue, returned now to its
proper place, albeit amid the rubble of the temple of Athene Polias.
True, too, new statues were erected on the rock. The most impressive,
perhaps created in response to one of Cimon's victories over Persia,
towered 30 feet (9 metres) tall, the work of the up-and-coming artist
Pheidias. Her head encased in a crested helmet, a spear resting
lightly against her shoulder, this bronze statue of Athene Promachos,
Athene Who Stands in the Front Line of Battle, gazed from the rock
towards the straits of Salamis, her right hand outstretched, winged
Victory alighting on her palm. Shown as an archetypal hoplite
warrior, Athene rested her left hand on her great round shield, its face
embossed with fighting figures – Lapiths fighting centaurs, those half-
man half-horse symbols of bedlam whom the Athenians may very
well have brought to mind when they saw Xerxes' eastern Ethiopians
with their horse-skull headdresses. The statue was so tall that the
spear tip, flashing in the sun, could be seen by sailors rounding
Sounion or speeding to Piraeus from the south.

Yet how Cimon must have ached to build on the Acropolis. How
irksome he could not. The terms of the Oath were clear. And yet…
There was nothing to prevent building on new sites. And there was
one Athenian hero who deserved a temple of his own, a hero who
(it was increasingly believed) had cleared the land of wrongdoers,
had freed his city from a tribute forced on them by foreigners, had
fought beside his people in his ghostly form at Marathon: Theseus,
who had died in exile on the island of Scyros and whose bones an
oracle was now insisting should be repatriated to his native Athens.

Cimon understood perfectly the power of grand theatrical
gesture and this was just the kind of opportunity he needed. For

drama and politics were intertwined. Later (468 BC) Cimon would use his power to destroy the reputation of the leading dramatist Aeschylus, whose previous play, *The Persians* (472 BC), had been sponsored by the son of his rival, Xanthippus. The episode is instructive:

> When Cimon and the other generals had entered the theatre and offered the customary libation to Dionysus, he forbade his colleagues to leave, but made them sit as judges ... They awarded the prize to [the newcomer] Sophocles, and it is recorded that Aeschylus was so resentful that he did not stay in Athens long before he decamped in anger to Sicily, where he died.[69]

Now though (475 BC), Cimon staged his own theatrical coup, a production of epic proportions. Using the oracle as an excuse to invade Scyros, he set his troops to scour the island for any evidence of Theseus' grave. Not unsurprisingly, given Cimon's enthusiasm for the project, his men soon found a sarcophagus containing a spear, a sword and a skeleton of quite heroic proportions. The quest had been successful. Theseus had been discovered.

With pomp and ceremony the casket containing the remains was conveyed in the official state trireme to Piraeus, where a crowd of cheering citizens

> greeted them with spectacular processions and sacrifices, as if the hero himself was coming home. He is buried in the centre of Athens ... and his tomb is a sanctuary for ... all the poor and persecuted who fear those with power, for, while he lived, Theseus was the protector of the needy and always listened with kindness to the requests of the poor.[70]

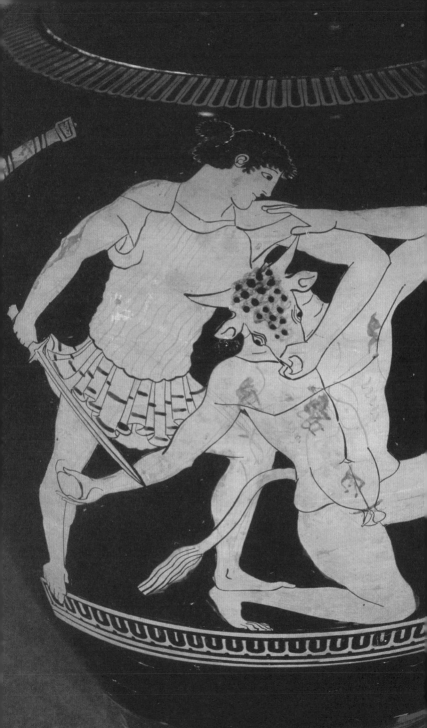

Or so Cimon would have it believed. Thanks to Pherecydes of Leros, Cimon's tame mythographer, the return of Theseus' bones coincided with a rewriting of Athenian history, in which the legendary hero was now a mix of benign tyrant and proto-democrat, a mirror image (some might have thought) of Cimon himself. Nor was this all. Twice-yearly sacrifices were instituted in Theseus' honour; the helmsmen of the fleet held an annual contest in memory of his pilot; and in the heart of Athens itself was built a temple, the Theseum, a new shrine to Athens' ancient son. And on its walls were brightly painted scenes from myths with which Theseus was associated, and which echoed eerily events from the recent past: the attack on the Acropolis by the barbarian Amazons; Theseus standing at his friend Peirithous' side to fight the centaurs (a scene which, of course, also graced the shield of Athene Promachos on the Acropolis); and Theseus himself retrieving a gold ring from the bottom of the sea, proof he was the true son of Poseidon, just as his people, the Athenians, were true sons of the sea.[71]

Elsewhere in Athens other buildings sprang up, in which parallels between mythology and real history were drawn. At the northern boundary of the Agora, a long, two-storied *stoa* was erected, an arcade to house offices and shops, complete with a colonnaded portico. The Athenians called it the Painted Stoa, for hanging on its walls were painted panels, whose subject matter had once more been chosen carefully. Beside a painting showing Theseus and the Athenians fighting Amazons was a depiction of the Sack of Troy, the city whose destruction Xerxes had once vowed to avenge. And next to that, in a telling juxtaposition, was a depiction of the battle of Marathon. The second-century AD traveller Pausanias records:

> The Plataeans and the men of Attica are confronting
> the barbarians. The outcome is in the balance. But

Opposite Theseus about to despatch the barbaric Minotaur – one of the scenes shown on the walls of Cimon's Theseum. Red-figured *stamnos* (for storing liquid). Attica, Greece, 490–480 BC. H. 31 cm.

in the eye of the fighting the barbarians are fleeing,
shoving one another into the marsh. On the right
are the Persian ships and the Greeks cutting down
the barbarians as they try to reach them. The hero,
Marathon, after whom the plain is named, stands
with them, and Theseus is rising from the ground.
Athene is there, too, and Heracles ... You can clearly
make out, also, the general Miltiades.[72]

For no one must forget that Athens' victory had been won thanks
to the brilliance of Cimon's father.

Athens was becoming truly great; or, at least, she was becoming
truly powerful. At the suggestion of the Ionians, still reeling from
Sparta's proposal that they abandon their cities, the loose coalition
of allies formed to fight the Persians was formalized into a League.
At its head was Athens, but its spiritual heart and administrative
centre was the sacred island of Delos. Here on the shoreline, in a
solemn ceremony, each of the League's members bound themselves
in turn to Athens, sealing their oath to wage total war against the
Persians by casting bars of red-hot iron into the spitting sea (477
BC).[73] At Delos, too, were calculated the annual contributions in both
ships and money that each member of the League must make in
order to ensure the strength and maintenance of the fleet on which
success depended. The money, they agreed, would be transferred to
Delos every year and entrusted to the care of ten Hellanotamiae or
'Treasurers of the Greeks'. All of whom would be Athenian.

For six years, the League pursued its aims with a quite
remarkable unity of purpose. Cities that still harboured Persian
garrisons were attacked and defeated, while islands (like Scyros)
that were perceived as threatening safe passage across sea lanes
were mercilessly subjugated. But when Naxos, always an important
bellwether, announced its intention of leaving the League

(471 BC), the true nature of the alliance became apparent.
Thucydides, clear-eyed and concise, reports: 'Athens attacked,
and, at the end of a siege, Naxos was forced back into the alliance.'
He continues:

> This approach was followed with other allies in similar
> circumstances. Athens required total compliance with
> the rules and made itself most unpopular by imposing
> heavy pressure on allies who were unaccustomed and
> reluctant to make such sacrifices ... Reluctant to go

Above The reconstructed Stoa of Attalus commands the eastern flank of
Athens' Agora.

to fight abroad themselves, many member states had agreed to have their contribution calculated in such a way that rather than provide ships they should contribute their equivalent in money. As a result, they funded the growing strength of Athens' navy, so, when they revolted, they invariably found that they were poorly armed and had no experience of fighting.[74]

Throughout the next decade (471–461 BC), thanks to both the resolute leadership of Cimon and her tight hold on the League, Athens' dominance in the Aegean became ever stronger. Gradually but inexorably what had begun as an alliance between equals became an Athenian empire. Amid rumours that Xerxes was preparing a fresh invasion of the Greek mainland, Cimon led his troops to a double victory against the Persians by land and sea near the mouth of the Eurymedon in southern Turkey.[75] Demoralized, the Persians abandoned their ambitions for a new assault on Greece, and the next year Xerxes was assassinated in a palace coup. In Athens and the allied states there was much rejoicing.

Yet for Cimon, too, time was running out. An attempt to help the Spartans crush a slave rebellion backfired. The Spartans, not trusting the Athenians, sent them home. As a result,

the army returned to Athens furious, and initiated a very public revenge against any who supported Sparta, and especially Cimon.[76]

Despite all his handouts and popular largesse, Cimon was perceived by many as favouring the interests of the landed aristocracy. Opposing his faction was another group of politicians who, although from equally privileged backgrounds, took greater care to favour the People. Among these populists was a member of the Alcmaeonidae, the son of Cimon's enemy Xanthippus, a young man (still in his early thirties) blessed with a heady mix of wealth, confidence, intelligence and eloquence. His name was Pericles.

Already, he and Cimon had clashed in court, when (in a repeat of their fathers' law case) Pericles had prosecuted Cimon on a charge of misconduct during a military campaign. Cimon had been acquitted, but now (461 BC), he was not to be so fortunate.

The constitution of Athens allowed that from time to time a vote might be taken to expel for a period of ten years any politician who seemed too powerful or potentially tyrannical. During this exile his property was held in trust, but when it was over he could return to Athens with no stigma to his name. The mechanism was known as ostracism, because each citizen would write or scratch the name of his chosen victim on a piece of broken pot (or *ostracon*), before casting it into the voting urn. Yet it was a process fraught with potential risk. Ten years earlier, Themistocles, father of the Athenian navy and hero of Salamis, had been ostracized, and had ended up fleeing to (of all places) Persia. There he had been granted wealth and land and now he was giving the enemy advice on how best to deal with Greece.

With the humiliation of Cimon's Spartan debacle fresh in the minds of all, Pericles and his allies moved swiftly. In early 461 BC, Cimon was ostracized. The way lay open for a change of policy. In fact, Cimon's populist opponents had already been flexing their muscles. In 462 BC their leader, Ephialtes, had built on his success as a general three years earlier to transfer important powers from the aristocrats to the People. But, only months after Cimon's ostracism and before he could weaken the patricians' authority still further, Ephialtes was set upon and murdered, his body left bleeding in the street.[77] His assassins were never identified.

Ephialtes' place was filled by the aggressively patriotic and

powerfully persuasive Pericles. Pericles' first years as effective leader of the Athenian democracy saw conflict erupt across the Aegean. In Egypt, an Athenian task force found itself supporting a revolt against the Persians. Meanwhile, closer to home, cities like Sparta, Corinth and Thebes had for some time been looking with alarm

Above The remains of ancient Sparta are dominated by the snow-capped peaks of Mount Taygetus.

at Athens' growing political and economic power, and now their discontent erupted into full-blown war.

For ten years, bloody fighting between Greek states ebbed and flowed across the mainland. Campaigns were launched and cities captured by both sides. For Athens, despite defeats and setbacks, the war provided a welcome chance to annex nearby territories: Megara, by land a useful buffer, her port a valuable launch pad from which to attack Corinth; Aegina, clearly visible from the Acropolis, in Pericles' own words 'the eyesore of Piraeus', which had once capitulated to the Persians and had long been Athens' enemy.

By the time Cimon returned home (451 BC), he found that the mood in Athens had changed significantly. The appearance of his city had changed, too. Attacks on Attica had exposed how vulnerable Athens was to siege. A generation earlier, after the Persian Wars and as part of his policy for strengthening his city as a maritime power, Themistocles had urged his fellow citizens not to rebuild ruined Athens where she had once stood, but to relocate from the slopes of the Acropolis to Piraeus, where it would be so much easier to ensure uninterrupted access to food supplies by sea. At the time, his proposals had been shouted down – the Acropolis was Athens' heart! – but now, too late, they seemed eminently sensible. Years before, Cimon had already begun to construct a defensible wall linking Athens and the anchorage at Phalerum (462 BC). Now, a second set of two parallel walls was built, 5 miles (8 km) in length, stretching from the ramparts of Athens down to Piraeus. Between the walls was a broad and well-protected avenue, an artery through which supplies could flow uninterrupted, even in times of siege, from the sea straight into Athens.

But this was not the only evidence of change which greeted Cimon on his return. Surrounding Athens with new fortifications may have contributed to a realization of how vulnerable her island treasury – or rather that of the League – might possibly become. The expedition which Pericles had sent against the Persians in Egypt in 454 BC had suffered a catastrophic loss of men and ships. As news of the sheer scale of the disaster swept through the Aegean, Ionians and islanders were gripped with panic. What if the Persians returned? What if their victory against Greeks in Egypt galvanized them into action? And with mainland Greece locked in self-destructive conflict, what better time than now for the Great King to invade?

Suddenly even Delos seemed exposed. True, Xerxes had spared its temples in his voyage of plunder, but how tempting now the treasury must seem. How vulnerable. Or so, at least, Athens' envoys to the member states would make out. Hastily the island's strong rooms were emptied of their riches. Efficiently the crates were carried to the ships. The inventories were checked, the anchors weighed, and in one swift, well-oiled operation the financial capital of the Delian League was transferred to Athens. And why not? Athens, after all, was providing the security for the League. It was only appropriate that she should house its money. (Though not without charge. From now on, one-sixtieth of all the League's contributions would be donated to Athene as a fee for their safekeeping.)

Reminded of the reality of the Persian threat, many in Athens welcomed Cimon's return as an opportunity to discuss peace terms with the Spartans and their Peloponnesian allies. Within months, he had negotiated a five-year truce, an opportunity for Athens to regroup and carry the war back across the Aegean and to Persian shores. Wasting no time, Cimon sailed with an army from Piraeus, setting course south-east for Cyprus and Egypt.

When the ships returned months later, they brought reports from Cyprus of victories and death. The death was Cimon's, killed in the fighting by the walls of Citium, though his enemies said he had died of sickness.[78] The victories came later, one over the Persian fleet at sea, the other the same day over the Persian army on the shoreline of a Cypriot city which shared its name with an island already famous in Greek history: Salamis (450 BC). The oracle delivered to the Athenian envoys, trembling in the temple of Apollo at Delphi thirty years before, that Salamis would be the cause of death to women's sons, had come doubly to pass.

Even the Persians knew the game was up. Artaxerxes, the Great

King, announced that it was time to come to terms. An embassy
from Athens made its long way east to Susa. At its head was Cimon's
brother-in-law, Callias. The subsequent peace treaty bore his name.[79]
The long history of conflict which had started with the revolt of the
Ionian cities and the burning of the temple of Cybele in Sardis was
at an end. The slate had been wiped clean. And with it, or so
Athenians like Pericles would argue, had been removed the obligations
imposed by the Oath of Plataea. For surely the oath applied only as
long as there was a Persian threat. And it had been so limiting.
For years, Athenians had been cruelly forced to endure the sight of
their blackened Acropolis, its temples twisted out of all recognition.
And not only the Athenians. Their gods had endured it, too.

And this at a time when other cities, which had not suffered as
Athens had, were free to build whatever temples they had wanted
in whatever places they chose! How it had rankled when Athenians
had gone to the Olympic Games and over five Olympiads
(472–456 BC) had been obliged to watch the huge new temple of
Olympian Zeus rise from its platform in the sanctuary. With a
length of 210 feet (64.12 metres) and breadth of 91 feet (27.68
metres), it had become the largest temple on the mainland. It was,
moreover, roofed with thin slabs of marble from the Attic quarries
of Pentelicon. Painted and picked out in gold, it was, in short,
magnificent: a mainland rival to the fabulously wealthy temple
of Artemis at Ephesus. But at Olympia. Not Athens.

As Pericles and his allies recovered from the brief eclipse which
they had suffered on Cimon's return, their eyes strayed more than
once to the Acropolis. With the Peace of Callias, Athens needed a new
purpose and a new beginning, a new symbol of her greatness and her
boundless ambitions. Swiftly Pericles tried to convene a conference of
all the Greeks, a Panhellenic Congress, to discuss not only the policing
of the now Persian-free seas but the rebuilding of the temples burnt
by the 'babarians'. High-handedly the Spartans turned him down.

For them the sea held little interest, and the Persians had destroyed no temples in their territories. Besides, to meet in Athens would be to pander to that city's claim to be the leader of the Greeks. Plans for the Congress were abandoned as quickly as they had been made. Not that it mattered much. It would have been a mere formality. For, whatever might have been decided there, Pericles and his entourage of all the brightest and the best in Athens knew the time had come to demonstrate to all the world that their city could surpass its rivals, not just in battle, but in architecture, too. The time had come to build the Parthenon.

Part 2
The Parthenon

Chapter 4

Athens Redux

Fix your eyes every day on the greatness of
Athens as she really is, and become her lover.[80]

If the decision to rebuild the ruined temples on the Athenian
Acropolis had been postponed for thirty years, once it had been
made and ratified, the project quickly took on a momentum of its
own. Money was not a problem. Colonnaded temples, such as the
Parthenon would be, still remained among the most expensive of all
public buildings, but, with a seemingly endless revenue flooding into
the treasury each year from the contributions of the Delian League,
not to mention from war booty or the mines at Laurium, and with
10,000 silver talents already in its vaults, Athens' economy had
never been more buoyant.[81] Besides, in accordance with the terms
of its foundation, a sixtieth of the League's contributions had been
ring-fenced as a donation to Athene (see p. 99) – and how better to
use that donation than by raising temples in her honour?

For the Athenians, perhaps the most poignant site in all their
city, the site most redolent of defeat and victory, was in the southern
quadrant of the Acropolis. Here was the platform on which, in the
mid-sixth century BC in the time of the tyrants, the first limestone
temple of Athene had been built. Here too, after Marathon, its proudly
democratic yet ill-starred successor had been begun, only to be burnt by
Xerxes. Here overlooking the new city, resurrected from the rubble of

Opposite Looking from the approach to Pynx Hill, the Parthenon
dominates the Athenian Acropolis.

destruction and now ruling much of the Greek world, would be sited the first of Pericles' new temples. Here would be built the Parthenon.

On the platform on which the temple would be raised, and all around it, the ground was cleared and levelled. To the south, thanks to Cimon's new retaining wall, the terrace had been widened, allowing greater breathing space around the temple. To the north, the platform itself was extended – for the Parthenon was to be larger than either of its two predecessors. And not only them. Crucially, given Athens' international ambitions, the Parthenon would surpass in size its mainland rival, the temple of Zeus at Olympia, consecrated only nine years earlier. Some 15 feet (5 metres) longer and 9 feet (3 metres) wider than the Olympian temple, the Parthenon would be the largest sacred building in mainland Greece.

The enlargement of the platform had another important impact on the Parthenon's design. It meant that a relationship of 9:4 could be established between its long sides and its short (228 feet x 101 feet or 69.5 metres x 30.88 metres), a ratio that was applied elsewhere in the temple. Thus the relationship of width to height of both facades is also 9:4, as is the ratio of the distance between the middle of each column and the middle of the next (the so-called interaxial measurement of 10 feet 6 inches or 3.2 metres) to the diameter of the column bases (6 feet 3 inches or 1.9 metres). Because this ratio appeared throughout such key components of the building, it added to the Parthenon's overall impression of harmony, contributing significantly to its appearance of perfection, of a temple designed to contain something miraculous.

For, in recognition of her role as Athens' saviour, it was intended from the start that the Parthenon should house a truly awe-inspiring statue of the goddess. Not the ancient *xoanon*, the olive-wood statue given by the gods in the days of King Erechtheus, smuggled off to Salamis and safety when the Persians came, and now perhaps housed in a temporary shrine amid the rubble, for such was the sanctity of this venerable object that in time a new temple of Athene Polias would be built to house it. But the Parthenon, occupying the same physical space as the temple started after Marathon and designed, like it, to glorify its city's victories in battle against Persia, required a statue on an altogether different scale, larger even than the bronze Athene Promachos which gazed out from the Acropolis west to Salamis (see p. 88). Standing in the half-light of the Parthenon's echoing inner chamber, the new statue would face east towards Persia, a sister to the Promachos, but much more lavish. For it would be veneered with those most precious of commodities, ivory and gold. Raised on an elaborately carved base, this likeness of the warrior goddess with her glittering shield and helmet would soar 40 feet (12 metres), to tower in majesty above all who approached it. And because the Promachos was already such a powerful symbol of both Athens' and Athene's strength, it was clear that the same sculptor must be commissioned to create the statue for the Parthenon. So, with Pericles perhaps having to bite back some irritation that the man he was about to hire had been the favourite sculptor of his rival Cimon, the representatives of the Athenian People made their approach to Pheidias.

Pheidias was clearly the most outstanding candidate. Already his portfolio was second to none. There was not just the Athene Promachos. Across Greece, other statues, too, professed his genius, not least at Delphi. On the sacred way which wound up to the temple of Apollo, built there years before by the exiled Alcmaeonidae, a quite extraordinary statue group had been erected after Marathon, funded by tithes raised from the booty looted from the battlefield.

> They show Athene and Apollo, and Miltiades (one
> of the generals), as well as divine heroes: Erechtheus,

> Cecrops, Pandion, Leos and Antiochus ... as well
> as Aegeus and Acamas (one of the sons of Theseus)
> ... There are also Codrus, son of Melanthus, and
> Theseus and Neleus ... All are by Pheidias.[82]

It was a panoply of Athenian heroes, ancient and contemporary,
a manifesto of how Athens' power was built on a long tradition
of bravery and sacrifice, of which Marathon was but a recent link
in an enduring chain. That it included Miltiades among the gods
and heroes was not meant as any slight towards his enemies the
Alcmaeonidae (or so it could now be argued). Rather it provided
public recognition that it was thanks to Miltiades' decision to attack
against all odds that Athens had won victory at Marathon. In this
sculptural group at Delphi, Pheidias had demonstrated a profound
understanding of the symbolic power of that heroic battle, and
now, on the site of the aborted temple begun in its aftermath, he
was to raise a monument which would forever both encapsulate
and celebrate the lasting legacy of Marathon.

With its cost of between 700 and 1,000 talents significantly
eclipsing that of the 470 talents required for the temple itself,[83] the
statue was to be the centrepiece of the new building. In addition,
it was decided early on that, just as a mathematical ratio should
bind the building itself together, many of the subjects shown on the
details of the statue within the inner chamber would be repeated on
the sculptures on the outside of the Parthenon. To achieve the unity
of artistic vision, Pheidias was contracted to mastermind the entire
project. This did not mean that he himself would supervise the
day-to-day building work. After all, he was not an architect. Instead,
that position seems to have been given to two men, Callicrates and
Ictinus. Little is known of either's work before the Parthenon, but of
the two Ictinus was perhaps the more inspired. Certainly the work
for which he was commissioned once the Parthenon was finished

suggests that he was held in high regard.

The exact professional relationship of the two architects remains unclear. Did they share responsibilities? Did Ictinus replace Callicrates, who was assigned to work on other less prestigious projects before the Parthenon was finished? Certainly some later authors would name only Ictinus as the building's architect.[84] And what, in fact, did a temple 'architect' actually do? Sadly, Ictinus' own treatise about the building of the Parthenon has not survived, but some 400 years later the influential Roman author Vitruvius did list the skills required by architects. They ranged from mathematics and arithmetic to optics and acoustics, embracing on the way both history and natural philosophy as well as property law and medicine.[85]

Surprisingly, however, the fifth-century BC architect does not appear to have provided a blueprint or a model for a building's overall design. Later and at other sites working drawings were carved on temple walls, showing details like the profiles of the column bases or the plans for ceiling coffers, but there is no evidence of any such design drawings for the Parthenon. Instead, the dimensions of the temple appear to have been laid out on the ground with the positioning on the platform of the lowest column drums. Here, without doubt, it was Pheidias' vision which reigned paramount. Thanks to its newly enlarged platform, the building was to have not six but eight columns on its east and west sides, and seventeen on the north and south. The extra width afforded by the two additional columns was crucial. Not only would it add majesty to the appearance of the finished building; it would enable the temple more readily to house a statue of the size envisaged by both Pheidias and Pericles.

With the lower column drums laid out, the shape of the new building was established. The columns themselves could now be put in place. On to the base drums would be raised the next, and then the next again, each joined to the last with hidden clamps of iron encased in lead to protect them from the sea air. For otherwise the salt would cause the iron to rust and so expand and fracture. With the placing of each marble drum, cut perfectly to match the drum below and anticipating the next drum which would be set above it, both the cooperation and the precision of a workforce toiling in harmony to a grand (if undrawn) design became apparent. The artistic vision may have belonged to Pheidias, but it could have been a metaphor for the political governance of Pericles himself. For, as Pericles intended, the project galvanized all Athens, involving citizens and slaves alike and imbuing them with a civic unity of purpose. As Plutarch writes:

> [Pericles'] intention was that those who remained at home should be enabled to share in Athens' wealth no less than those serving in the navy or the army or on guard duty in Attica.

Plutarch goes on to list the staggering statistics of both the materials required to build the temple and adorn the statue (many of them imported from overseas) and of the diversity of the workforce:

> The raw materials which would be used were: stone, bronze, ivory, gold, ebony and cypress-wood.
>
> The skills or crafts which moulded them were those of: carpenters, modellers, copper-smiths, stone-masons, dyers, gold-workers, ivory-workers, painters, embroiderers and engravers. Also the suppliers and hauliers of these materials, people such as: merchants, sailors, ships' pilots, wagon makers, handlers of oxen and drivers for everything that was brought in overland. Also: rope-makers, weavers, leatherworkers, roadbuilders and miners.

Each of these activities (like a general with dedicated troops under his own personal command) could draw on a dedicated battalion of unskilled workers, who worked in a junior role in the same way as an instrument is governed by the hand or the body or the soul. In this way, meeting such demands, Athens' wealth was rolled out far and wide and divided among every generation and class in the city.[86]

While, on the Acropolis, the platform and its surroundings had been being prepared, near the village of Icaria, where Thespis had once invented drama, around the marble quarries of Pentelicon,

Above Athenian metalworkers swelter in the heat of a forge. Black-figure *oinochoe* (wine jug). Attica, Greece, 500–475 BC. H. 26.7 cm.

12 miles (20 km) north-east of Athens, the countryside had been reverberating to the crack of rocks split by the pounding of iron hammer on iron wedge. This was the native marble from which the Parthenon was to be built. By the time the temple was finished, in a cloud of dust and chippings, more than 1,415 cubic metres (500,000 cubic feet) of the gleaming stone would have been hewn from the hillside. Once the gangs of labourers had cut out each heavy block, the marble would be roughly shaped according to its ultimate purpose: column drums rounded, building blocks squared, while any particularly special piece, identified by overseers as having the potential to be used in one of the decorative sculptures, was set aside perhaps to be examined by Pheidias himself.

Then began the marble's journey into Athens. This was best made in the baking months of high summer, from July to September, when the earth was hard and dry, and the roads more suited to the transportation of such heavy loads. Then, too, the oxen yoked to haul the groaning lumbering carts could be spared from their more normal duties ploughing the fields or transporting produce through the lanes of Attica. Down from the hillside, parched and loud with the drilling of cicadas, along the dusty highway, on through the well-guarded city gates, along streets cleared of stalls and traffic for their passing, and up the ramp on to the plateau, wagon upon four-wheeled wagon wound its way to deliver the rough-worked marble to the Acropolis. Here, too, their drivers faced a frenzy of activity, slaves and free men working side by side, each paid alike a drachma a day, labouring to turn the raw materials of stone and wood into a building of perfection.

Once all the outer columns were in place, the walls of the building proper could begin to rise. Ropes looped round lifting bosses, left protruding from the marble blocks for just this purpose, were attached to pulleys to allow the slabs to be winched into position. Once up, the bosses were removed to create a flat and even wall. So gradually, course by course, the temple's shell was built.

On the inside of the Parthenon a cross wall divided the building into two. On the east was the *cella*, the great nave of the temple itself, in which would be housed the gold and ivory statue of Athene. On the west side was a smaller chamber, whose purpose was to be no less important. For this was to be the treasury of Athens, where would be stored not only such valuable items as belonged to the state but the tribute gathered annually from the Delian League.

While all this heavy lifting work was going on, the masons high on their scaffolding may already have been working on the final finish of the columns. Perhaps the most specialized part of the process was the creation of a slightly convex curve about two-thirds of the way up the otherwise tapering column. The reason for this so-called *entasis* (or tension) is now debated. Without it might an optical illusion suggest that the column was in fact concave? Was *entasis* required to make the columns seem less severe? Or was the viewer meant to believe that the weight of the roof bearing down on them was causing the columns to bulge? Whatever the reason, *entasis*, extremely understated though it was and worked out to perfection, appeared throughout the Parthenon, as well as in many other Greek temples.

Even the platform upon which the Parthenon sat was not entirely flat, but rose (albeit imperceptibly) in the centre, a curvature of 4 inches (10 cm) on each of the two long sides, and of 2 inches (5 cm) on the short. Because the columns which the platform supported were all of a uniform height, this curvature translated itself upwards to the entablature as well, with the result that the entire building bowed slightly upwards in the middle. Once more, the reason for this refinement is disputed. It too may have been designed to counter an optical illusion that the building was sagging. Or to add dynamism to the temple by the elimination of straight lines. Or to mirror the curve of the horizon. Or simply to improve drainage.

Nor were the columns truly vertical. Rather, from their base they inclined delicately inwards (the four corner columns adjusted to accommodate their position so that they lent on the diagonal) at an angle so subtle that, were they to be extended, they would meet in the realm of the gods, between a mile and a quarter (2 km) and three miles (5 km) above the earth. And while the width of the outer columns and the distance between most of them was more or less the same, the corner columns were made 2 inches (5 cm) thicker and set closer to their neighbours, perhaps to add to an overall impression of solidity, or perhaps to counteract the glare resulting from the lack of wall behind them.

Now the masons working on the columns could chisel out the fluting, the symmetrical vertical grooves which ran up each column, taking the eye upwards and helping to create a unified appearance from each series of superimposed drums. Work on the fluting had started early in the process. In fact, the bottom few centimetres of each of the lowest column drums were fluted before they were even set in place. When the rest of the column had been raised, the masons worked to plumb lines, carving upwards to continue these first grooves all the way up to the capitals. In keeping with every mainland temple that had preceded it, the Parthenon's outer columns were of the Doric order. Broad and unfussy, regular and masculine, they suited both the building and the warlike Athene in whose honour it was built.

With the exoskeleton of columns now complete and the inner walls constructed and worked smooth, it was almost time to begin work on the roof. Because of width of the *cella* and the great distance which the roof beams would have otherwise to span (82 feet or 25 metres), two lateral rows, each of ten columns with one engaged column built into the east wall, were set in place along with a further row of five medial columns behind where the statue would stand at the west of the room (see illustration, p. 127). Lest these colonnades seem to dominate the *cella*, they needed to be slimmer than those on the outside of the building. Hence the columns were double-tiered, with those above being shorter and narrower than those below. Within the smaller west room, where the treasury was housed, and where an appearance of airiness was not at such a premium, the roof beams were supported by four single columns, but whereas every other column in the Parthenon was Doric, these four alone were Ionic. Perhaps it was because Ionic columns were more slender and took up less room that they were used here in the treasury. Or perhaps it was a statement of *realpolitik*: that Athens' wealth was built on the money of its Ionian 'allies'.

Before the roof beams could be fitted there was one final thing to do: the entablature above the columns needed to be set in place. And because they formed an essential part of this entablature, it was now that the first of the sculptures of the Parthenon were hoisted up into position. Now for the first time, observers could begin to see the type of imagery with which Pheidias meant the temple to be adorned.

These first sculptures were the metopes, discrete blocks carved in high relief, each containing one, two or at most three figures, depicting, for the most part, scenes from mythology. Approach the unfinished building from the west, as the drivers of the ox-carts did, and you would see represented high in front of you (just as it was not only on the Artemisium in Ephesus but in Athens in the Painted Stoa and on Cimon's Theseum) the battle of the Amazons and Greeks. But on the Parthenon its placing was particularly apt. For the legendary struggle had taken place here on this very rock, when, like the Persians in recent times, the implacable warrior women had launched their attack on the Acropolis and had been beaten off by the Athenians.[87]

Since the victory at Salamis, whose bay these metopes faced, the legend of the Amazons may have acquired a new layer of

meaning in the Athenian mind. After all, it was at Salamis that all their preconceptions of the Persians had been proven justified. For, xenophobic as Athens was at the best of times, its citizens considered these easterners to be effeminate. For one thing, they wore trousers – something no virile self-respecting Greek would dream of. And it had been at Salamis that Xerxes, praising Queen Artemisia too hastily, had uttered those telling words, 'My women have turned into men, my men into women!' (see p. 80). Perhaps these Amazons on the metopes of the west front were reminders of that very queen. The conflict on the sculptures was as yet unresolved. Indeed, the Amazons, whose queen was perhaps shown riding on a rearing horse on the left-most metope, seemed about to be victorious. Only one of the metopes on the far right seemed to

Above The north-east corner of the Parthenon today, showing the pediment adorned with (casts of) Selene's horses above the entablature whose metopes show the battle of the gods and giants, including (r.) Athene's chariot.

show a Greek warrior triumphant. Elsewhere these sculptures, albeit still unpainted and not yet enhanced with the bronze shields and trappings with which they would eventually be fitted,[88] spoke vividly of the uncertainty of battle, of an outcome hanging in the balance.

The metopes on the north side showed the war at Troy. But curiously, as the viewer walked eastwards, it soon became apparent that the story was being played out in reverse. For first were shown the gods, among them Zeus and Hera, learning of the city's capture by the Greeks, while the chariot of the moon goddess, Selene, plunged into the morning sea. Here was the Trojan Aeneas escaping from the burning citadel, while from its temple the Greek hero Diomedes rescued the Palladium, Troy's ancient olive-wood statue of Athene, the twin of Athens' revered *xoanon*, which was worshipped so devoutly only yards away. As the scene unfolded backwards into time, Helen cowered at the altar, trying to escape her Spartan husband Menelaus' wrath as battle raged around them, while over at the far, east end the Greeks were disembarking from their ships as Athene leapt down from her chariot to join the fight. To the viewer, a pattern was already starting to emerge. Here once more was a battle between Greeks and foreigners. And not just any battle. After all, it was the Trojan War which Homer had immortalized in the *Iliad*, a poem which Peisistratus had tried to appropriate as Athens' own; it was the sack of Troy which could be seen now in the Painted Stoa next to a depiction of the victory at Marathon; and it was at Troy that Xerxes had vowed vengeance on the Greeks. And here on the metopes the Athenians could see not only a Greek victory, but one secured with the help of their gods – proof that not only might but righteousness was on their side.

Perhaps, as he walked towards the Parthenon's main doors, the viewer might have asked why Pheidias had chosen to show the Trojan War in reverse. In answer, he may have found any number of reasons: that the true 'front' of the temple was the east side, and that it was from here, not from the west, that the story unfolded; that, as he progressed east towards the Parthenon's main doors, the viewer was in some sense meant to be moving into a new reality; that as he studied the metopes he was not simply going back in time through a familiar story but entering an older and more rarified world, the world of the Olympian gods.

For, on the metopes which adorned the east side of the temple, the scene changed once again. Here the combatants were none other than the gods themselves. Here was their battle with the giants, the battle woven every year into Athene's robe by the elite young girls of Athens, a battle on a cosmic scale, the ultimate victory of the civilized over the barbaric. Approaching from the north, the viewer could identify the gods from their distinctive iconography or from the legends with which all Athens was familiar. First could be seen the sun god, Helios, driving his chariot from the sea into the skies, for like so many of the scenes shown on the Parthenon this battle began at dawn. Then came Hephaestus; then Aphrodite, goddess of desire; Apollo; Artemis lashing the galloping horses of her brother's chariot; Zeus, the king of the gods and his wife Hera, her chariot team of two winged horses rearing up, their front hooves thrashing in the air; Poseidon crushing a defeated giant beneath a torn-up mountain; Amphitrite; and Athene with winged Victory beside her; Ares, god of war; Dionysus, god of metamorphosis, a panther leaping next to him, his companion in the fight; and at the far end, Hermes, a fallen giant cowering at his feet.

The scene was so familiar and, though violent, nonetheless profoundly reassuring. There should be no doubt that its meaning was bound inextricably into the life of Athens. For this was the scene woven annually into Athene's robe – the *peplos* – the focus of the Panathenaic parade, which gave to each Athenian his proud identity. Indeed, it would not be long before the comic author

Aristophanes proclaimed on stage that

> a good man is one worthy of his country and the
> *peplos.*[89]

As the viewer turned and walked down the long south side, he
would soon have realized that unlike the metopes on each of the
other three sides, the metopes on the south did not possess a unity

Above From the south side of the Parthenon a metope shows a centaur,
his left arm draped with a lion skin, rearing over a fallen Greek. Marble.
Athens, Greece, 447–438 BC. H. 134.5 cm.

of subject matter. Instead the majority (twenty-four out of thirty-two) showed the battle between the centaurs and the Lapiths, the same conflict which could be seen not only on the Artemisium at Ephesus and on the metopes of Zeus' temple at Olympia but in Athens' own Theseum and on the shield of Pheidias' statue of Athene Promachos on the Acropolis. Here on the Parthenon horse bodies reared on hind legs to lash out, hard horse hooves pummelling human limbs, the faces of the centaurs terrifying masks of savage inhumanity. But like the battle of the gods and Amazons, it had particular relevance for Athens, for among the human combatants was Athens' own great hero Theseus, himself perhaps shown on the sculptures, as he fought to stave off the centaurs' drunken barbarous attack on Lapith women at the wedding of his friend Peirithous. For this was a scene of sacrilege – the desecration of the sacred rite of marriage by creatures (otherwise intelligent) turned cruel and savage, maddened by drink and fury, using even the vessels of the sacred feast as weaponry. The centaurs' impious violence, subdued by Theseus, may be seen as a metaphor for that of the Persians, defeated by Theseus' descendents, the Athenians.

But positioned in the centre, flanked by the centaurs and Lapiths, were eight metopes where the subject matter was seemingly completely unrelated to these scenes of barbarism. For these showed scenes from fifth-century BC Athenian life – indeed scenes related to the Panathenaic Festival. Here was a musician with his *kithara* (a large stringed instrument), here wrestlers, here women and young girls standing by Athene's ancient *xoanon*, with others weaving at the loom what must undoubtedly have been the *peplos* given to the goddess at the festival. Why were they present, these testaments to contemporary life, among the conflicts of mythology? Perhaps the metopes which showed the centaurs and the Lapiths had been reused from an earlier unfinished building – but this does not explain why the sculptors, faced with having to create a further eight, did not carve them to the same theme. Surely the decision to include episodes linked to the city's greatest festival was not made on a whim. Rather, the singing and the games and the weaving of the *peplos*, positioned as they are with conflict swirling around them, seem deliberately to present an image of stability and certainty, the enduring power of civilization in the quiet eye of the storm.

Just as on the panels in the Painted Stoa down in the Agora, so here on the Parthenon the message was clear. On every side the metopes showed Greeks overcoming strange barbarians or Greek gods overcoming the primeval force of chaos. And although the conflict at Marathon was absent from the sculptures of the Parthenon, the spirit of the battle and of the Persian Wars pervaded everything. Just as in the mythical Trojan Wars or in the conflict between Greeks and Amazons or centaurs and Lapiths or even between the gods and giants, so in reality Greece and her deities had been triumphant. And this was thanks first and foremost, as it would always be remembered, to Athens' victories at Marathon and Salamis and to Athene's intervention on behalf of her beloved city.[90]

But despite the unity of purpose shown on the Parthenon's metopes – despite, indeed, the high degree of cooperation demonstrated by the huge diversity of artisans and builders at work on the temple – Athens herself was still riven by political factionalism. Pericles may have been powerful, but he still had ambitious enemies, and they were determined to use his building programme as a weapon against him. In many ways, he should have been an easy target. Despite his democratic pretensions, he remained aristocratic in the extreme, and he had a reputation for being aloof, if not downright antisocial. He seldom appeared in public. Unlike so many of his rivals, who courted the People at every opportunity, Pericles took care to speak in the Assembly only very rarely and on matters of the gravest importance.

> He was never seen walking in the streets – except that
> which led from his home to the Council Chamber.
> He declined every invitation to dinner, as well as to
> any kind of friendly or family gathering. Throughout
> his entire political career, he never once dined at the
> house of a friend.[91]

His appearance, when he *was* seen, did little to dispel these impressions of remoteness. In fact, if anything, it enhanced them, as he took care to comport himself in such a way that he seemed to be completely unemotional, cultivating

> not only a majesty of spirit and an august manner
> of speech (which was devoid of the vulgarity and
> shameless familiarity of populist oratory), but
> complete control of his expression, which never
> admitted any laughter, a serenity of gesture and an
> elegance in his clothing, which remained unruffled
> even as he delivered speeches, a strong mellifluous
> voice, and every other quality well calculated to
> impress his audience.[92]

Not for nothing did his admirers call him 'The Olympian'. To his detractors, however (and there were many, who believed with reason that he was harnessing the power of the People to promote his own patrician Alcmaeonid ends), Pericles seemed arrogant, disdainful, proud and supercilious, contemptuous of all around him.[93] To them, he was big-headed. Literally. For his head was 'somewhat long and out of all proportion',[94] a defect which he tried to hide whenever he could by wearing a military helmet, but which earned him less than complimentary nicknames.

Undoubtedly Pericles' skull housed an impressive brain, but his was a ferocious intellectualism, which even among many of his sharp-witted contemporaries seemed dangerously suspect. For he surrounded himself with a gilded coterie of some of the greatest and most subversive minds of his age: Herodotus, who had travelled far in his search for an understanding of the causes of the wars with Persia, and who was already formulating his discoveries in his new groundbreaking history; Sophocles, the playwright (once backed so spectacularly by Cimon), whose tragedies explored a world ruled by a divine order which was unknowable to man; and philosophers like Anaxagoras, who sought a rational explanation for natural phenomena and

> was the first man to reject Chance and Necessity and instead to establish pure Intelligence as the prime motivator of that law and order which pervades the Universe, and which sets apart those bodies which share common elements from an otherwise disordered chaos.[95]

The metopes of the Parthenon were a perfect illustration of Anaxagoras' philosophy.

To Pericles' political opponents the building works now under way were a gross misuse of public funds, a vanity project of the kind once so beloved by tyrants. As the city resounded to the hammering of chisels and the creak of cranes, discontented muttering spread through the Agora and Cerameicus, a groundswell of disaffection which threatened to lead not only to the project's cancellation but to Pericles' own ostracism. The situation called for action. Making one of his rare public appearances, Pericles (serenely) climbed the speaker's platform on Pnyx Hill, from where, above the Agora, the steep cliffs of the Acropolis could so easily be seen, and on their summit the wooden frame of scaffolding surrounding the still half-built Parthenon. The mood was ugly. The meeting started badly.

Addressing its concerns head-on, Pericles challenged his opponents. Had he, he demanded, spent too much? Given the public mood, he must have expected their reaction. A wall of noise, of jeering, catcalls, whistling and boos. 'Too much, and more!' Perhaps, too, he had rehearsed his answer. If the People were not willing to fund the building programme from the public purse, he said, he, Pericles, would pay for it himself. And dedicate all that he built in his own name.

It was a mighty gamble. Already the cost of the Parthenon was astronomical. By the time it was completed it would stand at 470 silver talents – considerably more than Athens' annual revenue,[96] and more than nine times the crippling fine which Pericles' father Xanthippus had imposed on Miltiades. And that was only for the temple. The statue of Athene would cost twice as much. Besides, elsewhere in Attica, other buildings were already taking shape (see Chapter 6). If the Assembly accepted Pericles' proposal, he would be ruined.

Not only that. His proposition could be seen as playing directly into his opponents' hands. By threatening to dedicate the buildings in his own name and not in that of the Athenian People, Pericles, heir to the fortune and the reputation of the aristocratic Alcmaeonidae, was coming dangerously close to identifying himself as the heir, too, of those former temple-builders Peisitratus and his hated sons Hipparchus and Hippias. He was laying himself open to the charge of allowing his true oligarchic colours to show through and harbouring an ambition for tyranny no less than that of Cylon. The Assembly was notoriously fickle. Its decision could go either way. For an anxious moment, the future not only of the building programme, or of Pericles' career, but of the very course of Athens' policies hung breathless in the balance. And then the People spoke. Or, rather, roared. The gamble had paid off.

> Maybe the People admired a gesture of such
> extravagance, or maybe they shared Pericles' ambition
> and they wanted to share in the prestige of his
> building programme. No matter why. To a man they
> shouted out, clamouring that he should take what he
> wanted from the treasury and spare no expense.[97]

The Athenian Assembly had accepted Pericles' terms. It had agreed
to acquiesce to his autocratic vision of democracy, in which he
and his elite circle could wield power as long as he did so with the
endorsement of the People and the People reaped the benefits.
It was an unwritten contract from which all might hope to profit.
Buoyed on a tidal wave of public approbation and knowing this time
that there was no more risk, Pericles put a second question to the
Assembly. Did the People, he demanded, wish to hold an ostracism?
Again, the answer came back loud and clear. They did! And when
the vote was taken, and the leader of the opposition was sent off
to exile, all residual resistance both to Pericles and to his policies
evaporated (444 BC).[98] For most of the next fifteen years, Pericles
would rule supreme, the unconstitutional monarch of Athens and
her empire, a beneficent tyrant over Athens' people. As the historian
Thucydides would comment, what was 'a democracy in name was
in fact government by its first citizen'.[99]

Meanwhile work on the Acropolis continued uninterrupted.
For the moment, until the roof was on, the metopes remained
unpainted, for there was still much building work to do. The marble
pediments (as yet unadorned with their statuary) were still to be put
in place. And then the roof. The great beams of cypress wood from
which the framework of the rafters would be fashioned had already
been cut and roughly shaped and shipped by sea to Athens' port
at Piraeus from Carpathus, the hot and mountainous island in the

south-east Aegean halfway between eastern Crete and Rhodes.

With these rafters in position, the thin slabs of translucent Parian marble that would replace the terracotta more usually used on temple roofs were hoisted up the scaffolding and hammered into place. Regular rectangular pantiles, the bottom of each overlapped the top of the one below it, their long sides covered by a line of corresponding ridge tiles. Only the temple of Zeus at Olympia had such a marble roof, and the quality of light which filtered through it was remarkable, casting a golden glow into the building's hushed interior. But the temple at Olympia as yet contained no statue. Athene's temple, on the other hand, soon would. While the teams of labourers and builders, masons and other artisans had been busy toiling on the Parthenon, in his studio (perhaps somewhere on the Acropolis) Pheidias too had been hard at work.

He had set himself a massive challenge: the construction of a huge self-standing statue, 40 feet (12 metres) tall (including its base), on a scale and budget unprecedented anywhere on the Greek mainland. The image of Athene was built around a wooden frame, faced in its entirety with ivory and gold, and adorned with precious metals, glass and stones. Like the temple which would house it, the statue required its own team of dedicated artisans as well as traders who would source the raw materials from across the Greek world and beyond.

Fortunately for Pheidias, the Athenians were no strangers to carpentry. Since the days of Themistocles they had been constructing triremes and the result was that the city and its dockyards were a rich repository of knowledge and experience. Both would now be put to good use. To create the statue's armature or hollow framework, Pheidias chose cypress and citrus woods, both sturdy and long-lasting, and well known for their resistance to insects and decay.[100] At its core was a massive central beam, 2 and a half feet (75 cm) by nearly 2 feet (54 cm) wide, set 14 inches (37 cm)

Above Pheidias' statue of Athene in its original setting may have looked like this replica from Nashville, Tennessee. Gilded plaster, Alan LeQuire, 1982–2002.

deep into the temple floor, and rising tall like a ship's mast to the full height of the statue. To this was attached the rest of the armature, as a later (Roman) writer put it:

> a riot of rods and poles and battens driven through it, beams and wedges and tar and clay – a veritable mishmash of unsightly stuff.[101]

Once the solidity of the framework could be relied upon, work could begin on the statue's shell. Because of the expense of the materials with which it would be faced and the expanse they would have to cover, only a thin veneer of gold and ivory was to be used, beneath which the main body of the statue would be made of wood. Like the Athene Promachos, this new Athene (called the Parthenos, or Virgin) would show the goddess, helmeted and armed with both a shield and spear, stretching her right hand out towards her worshippers. And in that right hand, she would hold a life-sized statue of winged Victory.

As the component parts took shape, a shipment of elephant tusks arrived at the Acropolis. Ivory had long been used in statues of the gods, and experts knew well the best way to prepare it. Because elephant tusks are composed of layers, those layers could be delicately cut and unrolled to form thin strips up to 40 feet (12 metres) long, which could then be softened either through heating them in a flame, or through boiling them in beer.[102] The softened ivory could then be moulded round the statue's face, arms, hands and feet. When it was smoothed and polished, it radiated with a life-like glow. It had become Athene's flesh.

As for the gold, it too was applied as a thin and shimmering veneer, sheets held in place by tiny nails – on Athene's helmet, on her shield, her spear, her sandals, and on the deep folds of her robe which fell, so brilliant and lustrous, to her ankles. All the gold, weighing as it did some 40 talents (2,280 lbs; 1,034 kg), could be removed, for Pericles was adamant that even though it had been dedicated to the goddess, it could be melted down and used in times of trouble, as long as it was then replaced to the same – or to a greater – value.[103] Later, indeed, stories would begin to circulate that Pheidias himself had so contrived these sheets of gold, and that he had been forced to take them down and have them weighed to prove that he had not been guilty of embezzlement.[104]

For now, though, all that still lay in the future. Now was the time for the final adornment of the statue. If, as seems likely, Pheidias employed techniques which he would later use in making his great statue of the seated Zeus at Olympia, he now set his team to work on the details of silver, bronze and copper, of glass and brightly coloured stones, to catch the light, red, blue and green, and glint resplendent on Athene's robe. Final details, too, were needed for the Gorgon's head which grinned from the snake-fringed *aegis* atop Athene's breast, and for Athene's eyes, those grey and flashing eyes by which she was ubitquitously known. For, once those were in place, her lips stained red, a blush of pink massaged into her ivory cheeks, the statue was complete. And Pericles could view it.

Even knowing what to expect, it must have been breathtaking and even slightly terrifying. The Greeks believed that gods resided in their statues to the extent that the statue was in some way alive. The deadly oracle delivered before Salamis had spoken of statues trembling and oozing sweat as they contemplated the Persians' advance, and even five centuries later the urbane and worldly-wise Plutarch described how

> statues have been seen to sweat and weep and emit
> what seem like drops of blood… and it is possible that
> they may give forth sounds like moans or groans…[105]

Indeed, Pheidias' own sculpture of Zeus at Olympia was later heard to bellow as if in rage when workmen tried to move it from its temple.[106]

So now, despite his undoubted rationalism, Pericles may very well have thought that he was being shown into the presence not just of a colossal statue but of the goddess Athene herself. Perhaps Pheidias had chosen the time well, for at dawn, as the sun rose into the clear skies above Hymettus, its light drenched through the opened doors and caused the polished gold to blaze in its reflection. To the viewer, dwarfed in the echoing temple nave, craning his neck to gaze on the goddess' face, implacable, Olympian, it was a sight of utmost splendour. Clad in her golden helmet, decorated as it was with horses and with griffins, Athene stared out at the rising sun. The Gorgon at her breast stared, too, a ghastly and barbaric creature from mythology, which (legend told) could turn a man to stone, but now was tamed and defeated as all who had ever threatened the power of Athene had been tamed. And staring from Athene's outstretched hand, high above the viewer's head, winged Victory, herself some six feet (1.8 metres) tall, holding high a garland.

But theirs were not the only eyes which gazed out at the sun – and at the viewer. Resting against Athene's shoulder was her spear, and twisting and writhing round it was a serpent – Erichthonius, the snaky incarnation of Athens' one-time king, whose living embodiment was still worshipped every month with honey-cakes. By Athene's side there rested, too, her shield, the great round *hoplon*, and on it there were scenes of battles that by now were so familiar. On its interior appeared the battle of the gods and giants, repeated on the eastern metopes and on the woven robe presented to the olive statue every year. On the shield's face was the struggle of the Greeks against the Amazons. Perhaps as Pericles looked up at it he experienced a moment of anxiety. Tradition and propriety forbade the likeness of a living man to appear in temples. Yet later sightseers

Opposite Two figures fighting back to back at the bottom of Athene's shield (shown here in a Roman marble copy of the gold original) were believed to represent Pheidias (l.) and Pericles (r.). AD 200–300. H. W. 45.7 cm.

were adamant:

> Pheidias [had] carved the figure of himself, an elderly
> bald man raising up a stone in both his hands, and
> also … an especially good likeness of Pericles fighting
> an Amazon. Although the positioning of the hand
> holding a spear in front of Pericles' face seems cleverly
> intended to conceal the likeness, it can nonetheless be
> seen quite clearly from both sides.[107]

It had, of course, been Theseus who in legend had seen off the Amazons. Was Pheidias deliberately identifying Pericles with Athens' greatest hero, blurring the boundary between mythic saviour and contemporary statesman? And, if so, who had come up with the idea?

It was not only on the shield that the subject matter of the metopes could be seen to be repeated on the statue, for around the soles of Athene's sandals there appeared the battle of the centaurs and the Greeks. Three out of four of the struggles shown high on the outside of the temple had been integrated into the statue of the goddess. Only the war at Troy was missing. Yet the statue did contain a fourth set of sculptures, and one perhaps not unrelated to the Trojan War. For the statue of Athene was standing on a platform, some 3 feet (1 metre) high, inlaid into the facade of which was a scene of birth, the creation of Pandora, the world's first woman, the cause of misery for men – a woman every bit as beautiful, irresistible and destructive as Helen, whose abduction had led the Greek fleet east to Troy. Pericles and Pheidias and everyone in Athens knew the story well, how Pandora had been created by Hephaestus, a 'savage beauty', a 'beautiful evil', the archetype of

> all the lethal race and tribe of women, who dwell with men to their distress, no help in grinding poverty, only in wealth.[108]

Writing in the early seventh century BC, the poet Hesiod had described how Pandora had been made:

> Zeus commanded Hephaestus to mix earth with water, and to imbue it with a voice and movement, like the movement of a human being, to form a face like an immortal goddess, and to give it the beautiful body of

a virgin girl. Athene should teach it to weave; golden
Aphrodite should anoint her head with grace and
agonising strong desire and body-breaking care. Zeus
then ordered Hermes to give it deceit and the morals of
a bitch. Zeus spoke, and they obeyed him. Hephaestus
shaped earth, as ordered, into the body of a modest
girl; grey-eyed Athene presented her with a robe and
belt; god-like Seduction and the Graces gave golden
necklaces; and the Seasons wove spring flowers into a
garland for her hair. Hermes implanted lies, persuasive
words and cunning in her breast and named the girl
Pandora (All-Gifted), because the gods had given her
so many gifts to be the ruin of mankind.[109]

The story of how Pandora opened the great and mysterious *pithos*
(or storage jar) containing all the woes and pains of men and
allowed them to fly unchecked into the world, so that only Hope
clung bravely to the rim, was well known.

So, what did it mean, this setting of Pandora's birth on the
platform on which the statue stood? Was Pheidias suggesting a
parallel between his creation of the statue of Athene and the gods'
creation of Pandora? Would this new Athene be as destructive as
the world's first woman? Surely not. Or was he ignoring the
catastrophic side of Pandora altogether and presenting her, instead,
as the archetypal weaver (as she also was), the predecessor of the
girls of the Acropolis who wove the *peplos* each year for Athene's
olive statue? Or was she an allegory for the potentially destructive
beauty of the enquiring mind, a warning to Athenians of the limits
of their frail humanity?

Perhaps it was meant as an enigma: like a Greek tragedy, always
posing questions and never giving answers; like the Sphinx in the
myth of Oedipus which, with her riddle, forces all she meets to face

their own mortality. To the viewers, the scene of Pandora's birth would have been dwarfed by the great statue which towered over it. Yet it remained, a constant challenge, perhaps as much a mystery to them as it is to us – the creation of a beautifully destructive force, flanked by the rising of the sun and the setting of the moon, as the gods of Olympus watched over it.

Undoubtedly, the statue was set in place only once all the interior building work was complete and there was no longer any danger of its being damaged. Perhaps by now the high iron grilles had been secured between the pillars of the porches, east and west. Undoubtedly, already the heavy wooden doors too had been hung, two at the entrance to the *cella* and two at the entrance to the treasury, where they were reinforced by iron bars set deep inside the wood.[110]

From now on in the Parthenon would be hoarded the city's wealth. Here would be stockpiled the reserves from which her army and her navy could enlarge the territories over which they ruled.

Above The gods bring their gifts to adorn Pandora. Zeus (seated), Poseidon and Athene are on Pandora's left, Ares and Hermes on her right. Red-figure crater. Attica, Greece, *c*.460–450 BC. H. 49 cm.

But it was not just money that was kept here in the strongroom. Other treasures too were stored in cases or on shelves. In 422/1 BC, just ten years after the Parthenon's completion, an inventory included a golden garland, golden libation bowls, a gold drinking cup dedicated to Heracles, a silver and gilt mask, six Persian daggers, a gilded wooden incense burner, fifteen gilt shields, thirty-one shields covered in bronze, eight couches from Chios and ten from Miletus, a silver horse, a table inlaid with ivory, eight lyres (four made of ivory), an ivory and gilt flute case, drinking cups, an onyx stone set on a golden ring. The list goes on.[111] In the Parthenon, then, goddess and mammon ruled as equal partners. Spiritual power and economic might were combined.

The completion of the statue and of the building's structure (if not of all its sculptures) had been calculated to the strictest timetable. As the deadline drew nearer, the painters would be desperately trying to finish their exacting work. High up on the building's exterior, these skilled artisans were adding colour to the metopes – the backgrounds, a 'deep, rich, inky blue of lapis lazuli',[112] the figures themselves decorated in reds and blacks, perhaps with details picked out in gold leaf.

Perhaps gold leaf was applied to the column capitals, too, just as it was at Ephesus on the awe-inspiring temple of the goddess Artemis (which the Parthenon was clearly meant to rival). The capitals would almost certainly be painted. And above them on the smooth face of the marble, beneath the metopes and the now vibrantly coloured triglyphs, a geometric maze-like motif in red, gold and blue wove its way around the temple with an egg and dart motif below it picked out, clean, against the glowing marble. Below the painters, other teams of workers may well have been at work, applying coats of tinted wax or varnish to the columns and the walls, a protection from the elements, a reduction of the glare from the intense Athenian sun, a mellowing of the marble until it took on the appearance of thick and new-churned butter.[113]

It must have been a buzz of desperate activity. For already the month of Hecatombaion (July/August) was almost upon them. Time was running out. The Panathenaic Festival, which had dominated civic life since the time of Peisistratus, could not be postponed. And for this year's festival the building must be finished. For it was now, in 438 BC, on the day on which Greeks everywhere celebrated Athene's birth, that in Athens on the Acropolis a solemn service would be held to dedicate the Parthenon.

Above As this reconstruction shows, the upper courses of the Parthenon were originally lavishly painted in bold geometric patterns.

Chapter 5

Athens Bejewelled

When our work is over, we are in a position
to enjoy all kinds of recreation for our spirits.
There are various kinds of contests and
sacrifices held regularly throughout the year.[114]

Already, in the hours before the dawn, increasingly excited crowds
had been assembling on the level ground inside the city walls in
the narrow space between the two north-western gates. To the
left as you looked out from the city was the Sacred Gate, through
which, in a few weeks' time, throngs of pilgrims would file as they
did each September to begin their long procession to Eleusis and
its Mysteries; to the right, the Twin Tower Gate and the road to
the Academy, flanked just a short way off by the prestigious public
cemetery, the resting place of Athens' heroes and her war dead.

In fact, tombs lined both roads, adorned with sculpted figures
or with markers showing the likenesses of the deceased, many with
offerings laid out before them in memory or in placation of the
dead. It was a busy hub and often noisome, too, as a culvert beneath
the Sacred Gate carried not only the waters of the River Eridanus
but much of the city's sewage out of Athens.

Inside the walls, and pressing close up to them, this part of
Athens was the smoke-filled home of the city's booming potteries,
each equipped with a kiln capable of achieving the crucial

Opposite The Panathenaic Procession enters through the Propylaea on
to the Acropolis in this reconstruction by P. Connolly, 1998.

temperature of 950°C (1,742°F) required for firing the prized red-
and black-figure vases which found their way in tight-packed crates
south to North Africa, west across the Mediterranean and east to
Ionia and the Black Sea.

Only the square where the crowds were gathering was free
from buildings. Not that there was much space here on this August
morning. As the dawn grew closer, so did the levels of anticipation
rise. There were so many people. Old men clutching olive branches;
musicians in long gaudy gowns, tuning their lyres and warming
up their *auloi* (rasping reed instruments, ancestors of Armenia's
duduk or of the western oboe); animal handlers trying to calm
the cattle they had been grooming with such care throughout the
night; closely chaperoned young girls excited to be out of their
sequestered homes, thrilled and perhaps intimidated by the throng;
grooms yoking horses to their chariots, vehicles which could trace
their history back generations, lovingly maintained for occasions
just like this; even foreigners were here, draped in rich purple robes,
checking the cakes and honeycombs which they would carry on
their bronze and silver trays.

Among the old men, there may have been some who
remembered (or pretended that they did) a similar assembly seventy-
six years earlier, a similar atmosphere shattered by shouting and
the news of the assassination of Hipparchus. These men had seen
so much in one long lifetime: the tyrants driven out; the coming of
the Persians; the city burnt; the birth of empire; and the growth
of Athens' power under the leadership of Pericles. And now the
Parthenon, built, painted and ready to be consecrated.

It was the sixth day of the Great Panathenaia. Citizens and
foreign residents from Athens and from wider Attica had been
joined by visitors from city states across the empire and beyond:
politicians, merchants, athletes, all drawn by the prestige of the
event, many (no doubt) hoping to profit from their visit.

Over the eight days of the festival they would enjoy a wide variety of games and contests,[115] a wealth of competitions, some held in the Agora, some on the flat lands down towards the shore, still others out on the sea itself. For tomorrow, great crowds would throng the quayside at Piraeus to cheer a richly garlanded flotilla of ten ships, each crewed by young men from a different 'tribe' of Attica: their goal to row to victory around the headland to the harbour at Munychia, to win not only glory but a valuable prize. Unlike at other Games (the Olympics, for example), victors at the Panathenaic Festival won cash. The winning crew of oarsmen would receive 300 drachmas, plus a further 200 drachmas and three oxen for a feast to celebrate their victory; the crew that came second may have won 200 drachmas and two oxen – again, a departure from the Olympic norm, when only those who came first won anything at all.

At other events the winners received heavy 8.5 gallon (38.8 litre) amphorae, decorated on one side with the figure of Athene Promachos, complete with helmet, shield and spear, and on the other (frequently) with a representation of the contest for which the prize had been won. The content of these *amphorae* was deeply appropriate (and financially valuable, too, as it was quite in order to sell it subsequently): oil from olive trees sacred to Athene. Different values of prize were apportioned to each contest. At a time when an amphora of oil was worth 12 drachmas, the first and second prizes in the horse race were sixteen and four amphorae respectively; in the foot race for youths, it was sixty and twelve amphorae; while the victor in the contest for adult singers accompanied by the *kithara* was awarded not only 500 silver drachmas but a gold crown worth 1,000 drachmas. Even the singer who came fifth won a prize: 300 drachmas, close to the cash equivalent of the amphora awarded to the winner of the chariot race.[116]

This chariot race had been held on the fourth day of the Games in the hippodrome close to the sea, a thrilling event, so dangerous, so breathtaking, where lives could be lost in a split-second misjudgement, in the crashing of a chariot, beneath the pummelling of horses' hooves. Here, too, were held horse races, the young boy jockeys bareback, galloping, a blur of hooves, a haze of dust, and the hoarse and frantic clamour of the crowd. And on the seventh day (the same day as the boat race) was staged in the Agora another equestrian event, a special contest for charioteers and hoplites – the two-part *apobates* race in which at a given place the hoplite leapt from the moving chariot and ran in full armour to the finishing line. Here in the leafy Agora, beneath the plane trees planted by Cimon, crowds gathered on special wooden bleachers for other contests, too: foot races; the pentathlon; wrestling and boxing; and the dangerous and bloody *pankration*, the brutal all-in brawl in which only eye gouging and biting were forbidden.[117]

Not that every competition was athletic. There were musical events too: contests for singers accompanied on the *aulos* or lyre; contests for solo instrumentalists, as well; and contests for *pyrrhic* dancers, naked young men armed with shields who imitated

> tactics used to evade missiles and attacks by jumping, falling back and leaping up and crouching down – and their opposite: poses used to strike or to fire javelins or arrows or to administer many kinds of blow.[118]

There was even a male beauty contest, a team event whose rules we can only imagine, and whose prize included not just cash, but the award of shields and a place of honour in the Panathenaic procession.

But in the velvet darkness of the night before the procession took place, an event had been staged which would accord its victor an even greater honour. Greek days began at sunset, and now, as the sun had sunk behind Mount Aegaleus, the most sacred day in the

Athenian calendar had begun – the twenty-eighth day of the month
of Hecatombeion, the birthday of Athene.[119] There would be no
sleep for anyone in Athens. As evening fell, preparations for the 'All
Night Festival' were well under way. Apart from the feasting and
singing and the dancing and music which would resound throughout
the city from its streets and private houses, a race was run along
the straight road from the altar of Eros (Lust) at the entrance to the
Academy, on past the Demosion Sema, the public burial ground,
on through the Twin Tower Gate, up through the Agora and so to
the finishing line at the foot of the Acropolis, a distance of 1.5 miles

Above **A** charioteer and hoplite (helmeted and holding his round shield)
compete in an *apobates* race. From the south side of the Parthenon frieze.
Marble relief, Athens, Greece, 438–432 BC.

(2.5 km). It was a relay race, a torch race for ten teams, one for each of the ten tribes, each with a strength of forty runners, each of whom would sprint 65 yards (60 metres). The handover was crucial. Fumble it, and you would lose critical moments. Drop the torch or let the flame go out, and your whole team was disqualified. But come in first, and you won great glory, for it was from the winning torch that the altar fire on the Acropolis was lit for the sacrifice in honour of Athene's birthday.

And it was out across the city, past the looming Acropolis, that the crowds now ready by the gates were gazing, as the first pale

Above A fragmentary *aulos*-player (r.) plays while young men hoist and carry water jars on their shoulders. From the north side of the Parthenon frieze. Marble relief, Athens, Greece, 438–432 BC.

blush of light began to silhouette the hills and the stars began to fade. And then the sunrise. Dawn. The very moment of Athene's birth. And the procession in her honour could begin. Away from the Cerameicus and the tombs beyond the walls, the realms of Athens' dead, at a slow walking pace the column began to wind its way along the street between the potters' workshops. At its head were the city fathers, Pericles himself, his fellow generals, the ten tribal elders and the musicians, too, their melodies clearly audible, amplified as they were by the low walls of the houses on both sides. Then came the women, the girls with their jars of water, and those citizens who had been chosen to carry sacred offerings. Next, the cattle were led or driven on their way, heifers and great shambling oxen, their curved horns lustrous in the rising sun. And the chariots and charioteers. And then the rest of the procession.

As the multitude passed into the Agora, its route took a right turn and entered a landscape steeped in history. Behind now was the Painted Stoa, with its scenes of Marathon and Troy; to the right, half built, the temple to Hephaestus, whose axe blow had liberated Athene to let her spring in birth from Zeus' head. And straight ahead was the Acropolis, the Parthenon's new marble roof already gleaming in the daylight. On past the temporary bleachers, beneath Cimon's dusty plane trees, and now the road began to climb. Another right turn, and the route led past the Furies' shrine where once the rope protecting Cylon's followers had broken, allowing the Alcmaeonidae to butcher them; on past the Areopagus, which first the Amazons, then Xerxes' troops had occupied; and then a sharp turn left, and so onto the ramp which led up on to the Acropolis itself. Through the still-blackened Propylaea could be seen first Pheidias' statue of Athene Promachos, with the sun a halo behind her head. And when the procession reached the brow of the plateau, there beyond the still ruined sactuary of Artemis they saw it. In full view. For the first time. Perfect in its proportions, graceful

in its form, adorned with garlands slung between its pillars: the Parthenon. The first fruits of the new age of Athens victorious.

Yet for the moment it was not the Parthenon which was the focus of the procession. Rather, it was the small and unassuming statue displayed before its temporary quarters in the ruins of the temple of Athene Polias. The holiest of holies. The olive-wood Athene. As the column filed its way across the Acropolis, the Parthenon now rising to its right, the crowds fanned out, surrounding the makeshift

Above A heifer lowing at the skies is led to sacrifice. From the south side of the Parthenon frieze. Marble relief, Athens, Greece, 438–432 BC.

shrine and the altar between it and the new temple. Some no doubt
even stood on the Parthenon's marble steps to get a better view, as
the 100 oxen were led one by one up to the altar, their foreheads
sprinkled with white barley meal, their heads raised to the sky, their
throats sliced, and they collapsed, a spray of blood, a spasming of
hooves, onto the hard-baked earth. This was the *hecatomb*, the killing
of a hundred cattle, from which the month of Athene's birth took its
name: Hecatombeion.

The sacrifice done, it was time to perform the ceremony which
formed the very heart of the whole festival. Perhaps presided over
by Lysimache, the woman who would serve as Priestess of Athene
Polias until her death, aged ninety, many decades later, it was time to
make the presentation to the goddess, the gift of her new *peplos*, the
robe with its pattern of the battle of the gods and giants woven by
the chosen girls in the nine months before. As the musicians played
sacred music and the incense from the censers drifted high into the
air, the girls brought the folded *peplos* forward and offered it to the
Priestess of Athene Polias. Carefully the cloth was opened out, and
then wrapped reverentially around the statue. It was the most sacred
moment of the entire Athenian year, a moment of giving when the
covenant between Athens and its goddess was reaffirmed, a moment
in an endless cycle linking the city's past and future.

It must have been now that the Parthenon was consecrated.
No records have survived to suggest what might have happened.
Perhaps there were more sacrifices. Perhaps there were specially
commissioned hymns sung and dances performed. Maybe speeches
were made, too, and the great crowds filed in to view the statue,
gleaming fresh with gold and ivory. We do not know. At this,
arguably the greatest moment in the age of Periclean Athens, a
veil has descended over history. Knowledge of the ceremony might
answer many questions. How, for example, did Athenians view their
new building? As a conventional temple? Yet, elements normally

so crucial to a temple were oddly missing. Usually temples had an outside altar facing the main doors. The Parthenon did not. Instead, the altar faced the ruins of the temple of Athene Polias. Invariably, too, temples had dedicated priests or priestesses whose task it was to assist in the rituals and sacrifices with which the buildings were inextricably linked. Again, the Parthenon had no such priestesses. Lysimache was priestess of the temple of Athene Polias, not of the Parthenon. Even its name 'the Parthenon' would not be given for another hundred years, and even then it would be ambiguous. For in Greek 'Parthenon' has a genitive plural ending: it means 'The Temple of the Virgins', not of the one virgin, Athene.[120]

At the time of its consecration, the building may have had no official name. No sacrifices would be made here, no prayers offered to Athene Parthenos (the Virgin). Instead, flanked by marble inscriptions containing ever-growing lists of tribute exacted from the member states of Athens' empire, and adorned by sculptures of the triumph of civilization over barbarism, the Parthenon already seemed unique – not so much a temple as a statement. Of Athens' greatness. Of the sacrifices which its citizens had made in the name of liberty. A trophy to commemorate their hard-earned victory. As if Athens single-handedly had defeated Persia. As if Athens were the capital of the entire Greek world.

Yet there were still disgruntled voices. As the Athenians dispersed from the Acropolis, the ceremony done, some at least were doubtless dredging up the old charge which had been levelled by the now exiled opposition leader six years earlier (444 BC), that Pericles was turning chaste Athens into a wanton courtesan. It had been an allegation made more memorable because it was so vivid:

> The Greeks must think that this is an act of downright tyranny. Through contributions, wrung from them by force to fight against the Persians, we are gilding our

city, prettifying her like some preening woman putting
on a pretty face with her expensive stones and statues
and temples costing such vast amounts of money.[121]

And, indeed, to the more dour of Athens, the Parthenon invited
such invidious comparisons. Did not its stepped platform resemble
the high platform shoes beloved of courtesans? Did not the texture
of the creamy marble put those who gazed on it in mind of the
infamously pale cosmetics which a shameless woman rubbed into
her face? And as for the paintwork, the parallels with make-up were
much too obvious to mention.[122]

Perhaps these were the same people who had been spreading
salacious gossip about a culture of immorality that had pervaded the
Acropolis while the temple was being built. Gleefully disapproving
stories skipped through the streets of how

> Pheidias organized clandestine liaisons for Pericles
> with free-born Athenian women, when they made
> visits ostensibly to view the works of art. Comedians
> picked up on this, bombarding Pericles with any
> insinuation they could think of, coupling his name
> with that of the wife of his friend, and second-in-
> command of the army, Menippus. They even latched
> onto Pyrilampus' love of birds, accusing him (because
> of his friendship with Pericles) of giving his peacocks
> to any woman who had slept with Pericles.[123]

It was all good, knockabout fun. Yet, given the relentless spotlight
under which he had found himself for so many years, Pheidias
cannot but have felt a sense of some relief when he received a
commission from the trustees of the temple at Olympia. His statue
of Athene had impressed them. Now they wanted him to build them

another statue, a seated Zeus in gold and ivory, like his Athene,
40 feet (12 metres) tall. It would become a wonder of the world.[124]

But before Pheidias and his team could set off south-west for
Olympia, he still had work to complete in Athens. The sculptors
may not have required his personal supervision, but they did
need his input into the remaining works which would adorn the
Parthenon. For these, too, were to suggest the same thematic unity
that linked the statue and the metopes.

Because of the sheer volume and range of work to be completed,
several sculptors' studios were employed.[125] Some of the artists
worked in their own ateliers, or in temporary workshops on the
Acropolis itself. Others would need to work *in situ*, high up on
scaffolding around the building. Those in the workshops were
employed in sculpting the two pedimental groups, one for the west,
the other for the east. Some life-size and some larger, with a depth of
some 3 feet (0.9 metres) and rising to a maximum of 11 feet 6 inches
tall (3.5 metres) these figures were carved and painted in the round.
In a tradition dating back at least to the first temples on the Acropolis
over 100 years before, even the backs of the sculptures would be
finished to perfection, although such detail would be invisible from
the ground. These were, after all, statues dedicated to the gods, and
even if the human eye could not see everything, the gods knew all
and would not be satisfied with anything that fell short of the ideal.

The pedimental sculptures took six years (438–432 BC)[126] to carve
and paint before being carefully transported to the site and with all
the protection and precision that the winches and their workers could
afford them, raised delicately up into position. Here they were fixed
on to the pediment floors, many set in place with metal clamps to
fix them securely onto the walls and prevent them from crushing the
overhanging cornice which jutted out a full 2 feet (70 cm) or from
toppling forward to smash to the ground more than 40 feet (12 metres)
below. Once almost miraculously in place, the final finish would be

added, paintwork would be touched up or introduced and the metal ornaments (an axe head, spear tips, horses' manes and bridles) fixed and polished. When the scaffolding was at last removed the full force of these breathtaking sculptures, considered to this day as among the greatest ever made, could for the first time be appreciated.

The scene on the west pediment was set on the Acropolis itself.[127] In a laconic sentence Pausanias, who sadly had not quite found his stride when writing his account of Athens, summarizes what he saw: 'the west side shows Poseidon's contest with Athene for the land'. It must have been impressive. In the centre of the sculptural group, the two gods (Athene on the viewer's left, Poseidon on the right) had just arrived on the Acropolis, their clattering chariots and restive horses now reined in by attendants. The gods themselves, like *apobatai* in the Great Panathenaic Games, had leapt onto the ground. Already Poseidon had struck his trident's teeth onto the rock and the spring of water bubbled up. Athene, too, had worked her miracle. The olive tree was rooted in the soil; its silver leaves were rustling in the Attic breeze. The hostilities had set in train the series of events which, thanks to Cecrops' evidence, would see the land awarded to Athene. For Cecrops, too, was there (perhaps complete with snaky tail) as witness; and with him many of Athens' ancient heroes – Pandrosus and Erechtheus among them – while, at the outer edges, Athens' rivers, the Ilissus and Eridanus, flanked the dramatic scene as in reality they flowed past the Acropolis.

Like the metopes, the subject of the west pediment was the end of conflict. Yet, unlike them, it showed hostilities which in time would mellow into harmony. Although defeated, Poseidon would not abandon Attica. In fact, Athenians believed that it had been thanks to his help that their city had developed into so invincible a sea power – without him, Athens would never have managed to defeat the Persian fleet at Salamis. So now, here, facing Salamis, on the pediment of Athens' most prestigious temple, Poseidon was honoured equally with Athene.

On the Acropolis itself the signs of Athene and Poseidon's passion to make Athens their own were clearly visible. Only a few yards to the north, beyond the blackened temple of Athene Polias was the goddess' own olive tree, burnt in the Persian destruction, yet already the next morning sending out a fresh green shoot. And almost next to it, and just as holy, three grooves could be seen on the bare rock, the marks of Poseidon's trident, and beside them the salt well from which sometimes, so it was said, the worshipper could hear the booming of the sea. Just as the Persians had coveted the Acropolis, just as the Amazons had tried to take it, too (in the attack shown on the metopes immediately below this western pediment), so the gods had fought to have it. And in every case, Athene had been victorious. It was a dazzling vision. Not just in terms of art, but of propaganda, too.

The subject of the east pediment was equally remarkable. If on the western side the location of the action shown on both the pediment and metopes was the Athenian Acropolis, here the scene unfolded on

Above A local river god reclines, flanking the contest between Athene and Poseidon on the Parthenon's western pediment. Marble, Athens, Greece, 438–432 BC. H. (max.) 81.3 cm.

a truly cosmic scale. Set on Mount Olympus and flanked on one side by Helios, the sun god, whipping the fresh horses of his fiery chariot up into the heavens and on the other by the moon goddess, Selene, urging on her weary team as they sank exhausted down below the dark horizon, the sculptures showed the moment of Athene's birth. It was the dawn not only of a new day but of a brave new era – the day which the Athenians still celebrated in the Panathenaic procession to the Acropolis, which, too, began at dawn.

As on the western pediment, Zeus and Athene seem to have occupied the centre of the scene. Here, though, Poseidon was replaced by the blacksmith god, Hephaestus, still holding the axe with which he had cloven Zeus' head to allow Athene to spring out, already fully armed. The shockwaves of the birth were rippling out to affect all of the other figures looking on. To the left as you saw them, beside the horses of the sun, was a god, perhaps Dionysus (though he may be Heracles), and beside him, turned to watch the birth, three goddesses – Persephone, her mother Demeter, both seated, and standing beside them a figure thought to be Hecate – a triad of goddesses connected to the Underworld. On the right were other deities. Today we cannot identify them all with any certainty, but among them were Leto, Artemis and Aphrodite – goddesses of the upper world and of creation.[128]

If these identifications are correct, then, reading the pediment from left to right, the Athenian viewer may well have recognized an allegory: for if the reclining male was Dionysus, the figures on the left were all gods who (in part) were associated not only with the Underworld, but also (to their initiates at least) with the Eleusinian Mysteries of death and rebirth. There in the centre was, for an Athenian, the most significant of all births – Athene, the city's saviour and protectress, sprung from her father's head – while to the right were gods of order and the arts; of civilization; even, it might be thought, of empire. Like the course of the Panathenaic

Above Exhausted from its night's travails, one of the horses of the moon-goddess Selene's chariot team sinks below the waves. Sculpture from the eastern pediment of the Parthenon.

procession, in which, to mark this very birth, Athenians filed from the Cerameicus with its tombs beyond the wall up to the glowing heights of the Acropolis, the scene shown on this pediment was a journey out of darkness into light. A journey into creation.

Artistically, the dawn played another crucial role in the scene of Athene's birth. Every morning, as the sun rose high above Hymettus, its rays would strike this eastern pediment, the highest point on the Acropolis. And as they did so, on the Parthenon too there would be a spectacular eruption of light. For many of the figures were not simply painted, but enhanced with bronze, and with the coming of the daylight, they would flash and shimmer in the rising sun, a new awakening each morning, a new blaze of triumph.

Taken in context, the metopes affixed beneath the east pediment made even greater sense of this scene of Athene's birth. The metopes showed the battle of the gods and giants, another scene set at dawn. Indeed, the metope on the extreme right, where, now above it on the pediment, the chariot of the moon sank low beneath the earth, showed Helios the sun god urging his team of horses high into the sky. So, as the eye travelled down from pediment to metope, it was as if one day had ended and the next begun. And this next day was another day of victory, the victory over the giants, linked inextricably in the mind of every citizen with Athene herself – for this was the victory shown on the *peplos* they gave her on her birthday every year.

Perhaps there was yet another layer to this representation of the cycles of day and night, of birth and victory. In the most complete version of the story of the battle of the gods and giants which has come down to us, the mythographer Apollodorus describes (in characteristically leaden prose) how, in order to defeat the giants, Zeus had stopped the sun and moon dead in their tracks. For he had received an oracle,

> telling him that the giants would not be wiped out at the hand of gods, but only with the help of a mortal. When she heard this, Earth [herself a giant] looked for a herb which would prevent even a mortal from destroying the giants. So, Zeus ordered the Dawn and the Moon and the Sun not to shine, and, before anyone else could lay hands on it, he collected the herb himself, and through the agency of Athene he summoned Heracles to help.[129]

Had the gods not been victorious, there would have been no new dawn; and had Heracles, a human, at the bidding of Athene, not assisted them, the gods would not have been victorious. There could be no better illustration of the relationship between mankind and gods, or between Athens and her patron deity. For there was one more parallel which the Athenian onlooker would surely draw: the parallel of Marathon and of the Persian Wars. For their attack at Marathon had begun, too, at the moment of the dawn; and to the victory at Marathon could be assigned the rebirth of Athens' greatness. And who could forget the prophecy which, more than any, had given hope to their forefathers, when they had been forced to flee from the Acropolis down to their ships?

> Athene cannot completely win over the heart of
>   Olympian Zeus
> Though she begs him incessantly with many prayers
>   and all her guile ...
> Nonetheless, Zeus, the all-seeing, grants to Athene her
>   plea ...
> God-like Salamis, you will be the cause of death to
>   women's sons
> When the grain is scattered or the harvest gathered in.[130]

The bonds of covenant had gone full circle. Using Athene to intercede, Zeus had sought help from a mortal man to overcome the giants; using Athene once again to intercede, mortal Athenians had sought help from Zeus. And so had defeated the Persians.

On the pediments, as throughout the building – on the metopes and on the statue of Athene itself – the theme of victory was paramount, and with it (explicit or implied) the motif of Athens' partnership with the divine. Indeed, beside each of the base corners of both pediments cuttings in the marble would suggest that statues of winged Victories were fixed, their bodies stretching out into the void, apparently about to launch themselves in flight.[131]

Nor were these the only works of art to appear to spring out from the pediments, for on the apex of each there blossomed lavish marble flowers, their stems and leaves carved delicately in open tracery, their blooms conjoined to look like wings. Painted, with their details perhaps gilded, they may have risen almost 13 feet (4 metres) above the temple's highest point, a delicate crown to take the viewer's eye towards the skies and soften the otherwise hard lines. Along the long sides of the temple, at the edge of each row of marble ridge tiles, painted marble palmettes broke the otherwise undeviating horizontal plane, while at each corner beneath the bases of the soaring Victories, there jutted a lion headed water spout to carry off the rain. The Parthenon was the most lavishly decorated temple in all Greece.

For, as the sculptures for the pediments were being shaped and crafted on the ground, on scaffolding set up inside the temple's exoskeleton of columns close against the temple's outer wall, other teams of sculptors were striving to create what would become the most atypical and revolutionary of all the works of art associated with the Parthenon: a continuous (or Ionic) marble frieze running all the way around the building, and showing for the most part not a scene from distant mythology but a contemporary procession. Of mortals. Men and women, horses, sheep and oxen, in honour of the gods. Processions had appeared on earlier temples not least at Ephesus, where chariots and horses had paraded on the varied frieze adorning the temple of Artemis; and Athenian envoys may have seen processions carved into the walls of the palace of the Persian Great King at Persepolis, which had been built between 500 and 460 BC. But at Persepolis, the friezes had shown conquered subjects parading before their overlord, making offerings of

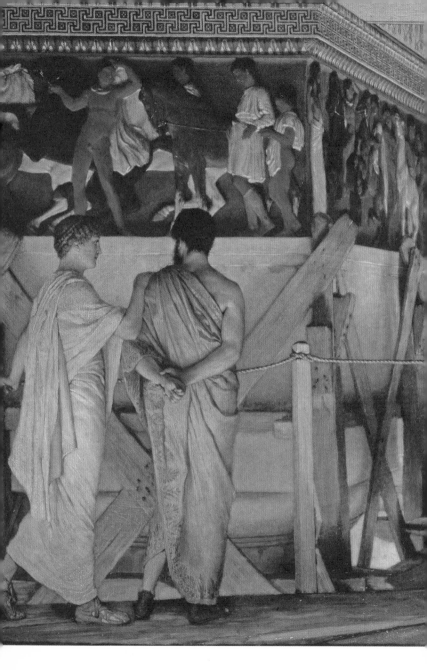

Above On high scaffolds, Pheidias shows the freshly painted Parthenon frieze to Pericles, accompanied by Aspasia and Alcibiades in this imaginative painting by Sir Lawrence Alma-Tadema. Oil on canvas, 1868, 72 × 110.5 cm.

obeisance which he, a mortal, had commanded. They glorified, in short, their people's subjugation. On the Parthenon, however, the new frieze would do something very different. It would explore the very soul of Athenian democracy.

Forty feet (12 metres) above floor level and carved in low relief, 3 inches (7.5 cm) deep at most, on marble blocks some 3 feet (1 metre) high and 524 feet (160 metres) in total length, the frieze ran on the two long sides along the top of the temple wall and on the shorter sides above the inner columns of the porches. Unlike the metopes and pediments, which could easily be viewed from a distance, the frieze could be seen only from relatively close to the temple. This made it, in a sense, more private. And this was appropriate. For, whereas the other sculptures had shown scenes of struggle or violence (even Athene's birth had involved an axe), the frieze displayed a vision of civic harmony, a united Athens processing in honour of her protecting gods.

In Homer's *Iliad*, the hero Achilles was presented with a great round shield, a *hoplon* crafted by Hephaestus, on which were worked scenes of a city's life in times of war and peace, the whole enclosed within an outer circle showing the sun and moon and stars.[132] In the Parthenon, Pheidias had translated Homer's vision into marble, and Achilles' shield into a temple. Elsewhere were scenes of struggle, but here on the frieze were shown the fruits of victory, the prosperity for which so many Athenians had sacrificed their lives at Marathon and at Plataea, at Salamis and Mount Mycale, at the Eurymedon and in so many other battles all across their world.

Perhaps, when the scaffolding had been removed, an Athenian who stared up at the frieze in the reflected mellow light, would have thought of these fallen heroes as he looked on the young riders with whom the procession began. For here, where he first saw them on the western side, were sculpted young men, idealized and beautiful, preparing for the ceremony, some controlling bucking horses, others adjusting boots and clothing, getting set to mount, others still on horseback guiding their excited steeds into position. All around them milled their grooms, while marshals tried to get the whole procession under way.

As he began to walk east along the temple's northern flank, the viewer saw that the riders, now assembled into ranks, some dressed in tunics, some bareheaded, some in caps with long ear-flaps, others almost naked, were urging their horses forward, first at a walk, then faster, trotting, cantering, but all the while controlled, careful not to gallop wildly, watched all the while and kept in check by stewards. Despite being in such low relief, the horsemen overlapped in such a way that they convincingly suggested great perspective, the angle of the horses' heads and hooves conveying remarkable variety and rhythm to the scene. Look at the bridles, affixed in metal to the marble, and you could almost hear them jangling.[133]

What would they have signified, these horsemen, to the Athenian who saw them for the first time? Certainly not the Panathenaic procession. Riders on horseback played no part in that parade. Perhaps he might have thought these riders represented the young elite of Attica, the *jeunesse dorée*, members of the upper class, the cavalry whose numbers Pericles had recently enlarged from 300 to 1,000,[134] and who regularly gave public displays of their equestrian skills on the flat ground of the Agora. Some decades later, Xenophon, himself a rider of some note, described his ideal display:

> For gods and mortals watching, the best thing is for the cavalry to ride around the Agora, beginning at the statues of Hermes [on the north side] and paying honour to all the gods whose shrines and statues they meet. Once they have completed a full circuit and are back at the statues of Hermes, it would be good if they galloped by regiment across [the Agora] to the Eleusinium [a shrine to the

Eleusinian deities at the south of the Agora]... After this gallop, they should retrace their steps, riding back to the statues at a walk. Such a display will enable gods and men alike to take pleasure, seeing all the agreeable sights provided by men on horseback.[135]

Elsewhere he writes of how both the officers leading their tribal divisions and the overall commander himself should ensure that all the horsemen under their leadership should provide an 'eye-catching spectacle'. It could almost be a description of the Parthenon frieze itself:

If the leading horse in a cavalry division is one which embodies all the virtues which attract praise to such a creature (one whose step is high and often prancing,

Above 'A constant clattering of hooves': cavalry divisions canter on the north side of the Parthenon frieze. Marble relief, Athens, Greece, 438–432 BC.

so that it covers little distance), clearly the rest of
the horses will follow at a walk. But there is nothing
impressive in such a spectacle. Rather, if you spur your
horse on and lead at a moderate pace, which shows a
spirited horse at its liveliest and best, there will be such
a constant clattering of hooves behind you and such
regular neighing and snorting that the entire division
(not just you) will make a magnificent display.[136]

Giving advice to an aspiring cavalry commander, Xenophon discusses
other such pageants, held near the Lyceum and the Academy as well
as in the Hippodrome, where the horsemen staged mock battles.
Sadly we have no direct evidence for such equestrian events in the
fifth century BC, but clearly they were soon to become part of the
fabric of Athenian life (Xenophon died in the late 350s BC).

Perhaps, though, for the fifth-century BC viewer, such an interpretation of the riders might have seemed too exclusive, too aristocratic. Maybe he saw in them the wider citizenry, elevated (thanks to art) to an ennobled state.[137] Or, if he was looking for a deeper meaning in their iconography, he may have considered how in other sculptures heroes were often shown associated with the horse – heroes in the ancient Greek sense, meaning men who had achieved a semi-divine status thanks to their deeds on earth. Men such as Heracles, who had fought on the side of the gods against the giants. Or Theseus, who had liberated Athens from the control of Crete. Or (and given the linkage in other contemporary artworks of scenes from mythology and recent history it is not inconceivable that the viewer might have made this connection) those who had sacrificed their lives driving off the Persians at Marathon and in the other battles of those wars. Perhaps this was the explanation of the blank expressions on the riders' faces, their anonymity in such stark contrast to the riotous individualism of their horses. Perhaps, then, this was not just a parade of the here and now, but a procession of the generations, past and present, united in their unselfish dedication to Athens and her way of life – generations of Athenians who, like their mythical ancestors, had sacrificed and still would sacrifice their lives in battle for their city.

As the viewer walked on, he saw that the riders had given way to four-horse chariots, each with a driver and a warrior in its car. These were the *apobatai*, the helmeted and shielded men who would jump down from their moving chariots to race each other to the line across the Agora in the Panathenaic Games, just as high on the west pediment Athene and Poseidon had vaulted from their chariots to try to be the first to step onto the Acropolis.

In front of the chariots walked the city elders, bearded and solemn, barefoot in long flowing robes, conversing with each other as they went. And then musicians, some strumming *kitharas*, others

playing the *aulos*, and young men, some with water pitchers
balanced on their shoulders, others with trays of honeycombs and
cake. And then the animal handlers, leading sheep and cattle –
another sign that this was not the Panathenaic parade, for there
only cattle would be sacrificed.

If the Athenian who by now had reached the far end of the
temple's northern flank had a companion who had been
walking in step with him but on the south, that friend would have
observed a similar but not identical layout. Here, too, horsemen –
ten ranks of six – gave way to chariots with *apobates*; here, too, were
elders and musicians, youths carrying water jars and trays, men
driving heifers.[138] But no sheep.

On the eastern side, where the iconography (thanks to the
subject matter of the metopes and pediment) seemed linked
somehow to Mount Olympus, the two wings of the procession
turned to face the centre. Here, for the first time, young women
could be seen, some carrying shallow bowls from which to pour
libations, others jugs, and others incense stands. And at the head
of the procession on both sides, two girls stood, stock still, staring,
watching the scene ahead of them. Beside them were ten men –
six to the left, four to the right – conversing, some leaning on sticks,
relaxed and casual. Who were these men? The ten heroes from
whom the tribes of Athens had been named? The ten generals
who led the army every year to battle? The generals of Marathon?
Or simply the city elders? Whoever they were, their attitudes of
informality were curious to say the least, for the scene which they
were flanking was populated by the most powerful beings in the
whole of the Greek world. For seated and shown twice the size of
the human beings in the parade, were the twelve gods of Olympus.

As the observer craned his neck to look at them, he would have
recognized each of the gods by their iconographic attributes.[139]
On the left was Hermes, with his traveller's hat and winged

sandals, not only the gods' messenger, but the conveyor of the
souls of all the dead down to the Underworld. Next, Dionysus,
the metal of the magic *thyrsus*-wand in his left hand glowing in the
reflected sunlight, leaning on Hermes' shoulder, twisting his body
round to watch the approaching procession. Beside him, their
legs overlapping, sat Demeter, her right hand held to her chin in
mourning, her left hand clutching the torch with which she lit her
path as she searched for her daughter Persephone. And next to her,
the war god Ares with his spear, clutching his right knee in both
hands, his bare feet raised from the ground, as he leant back, his
gaze focused on the procession in front of him.

Again, an Athenian would have made immediate connections.
For, reading left to right, these first four gods with which he was
presented were all connected somehow with the Underworld –
either, like Ares, through acts of killing or, like Hermes, through
guiding the dead beneath the earth, or, like Demeter and Dionysus,

Above The gods of Eleusis eagerly watch the approach of the procession,
while Hera turns to her husband Zeus (r.). From the east side of the
Parthenon frieze. Marble relief, Athens, Greece, 438–432 BC.

through their association with the enactment of the cycles of
death and rebirth at Eleusis. And all were watching eagerly as
the procession neared.

Which made the next scene all the stranger. For here was Iris,
like Hermes one of the gods' messengers, standing by Hera, wife
of Zeus, goddess of marriage, who was caught in mid gesture as she
turned her head away from the procession, raising her arms, her veil
held in both hands, an action of great ambiguity. Was she covering
or uncovering her head? In Greek art the gesture is used commonly
to show a bride as she veils her head on her wedding day, and
most of the metopes were connected in some way to marriage: the
marriage of Theseus to the Amazon Antiope; the broken marriage
of Helen and her husband Menelaus, which had led to the Trojan
War; the wedding of the Lapith bride interrupted by the centaur's
drunken violence. Yet there is something about Hera's gesture which
sets her curiously apart. For hers is the first face not turned towards

the oncoming procession. Rather she looks at her husband Zeus as
he lounges, relaxed, composed, omnipotent, his left hand resting on
the back of his low throne, on the arm of which is carved that most
enigmatic of all creatures, the sphinx.

To the right was another group of gods. Athene and Hephaestus,
the lame god clearly recognisable from his walking stick; Poseidon,
tapping Apollo on the shoulder, as the young god of music and the
arts looked round at him. Artemis, the virgin huntress, arranging
her dress carefully lest she reveal a breast, and Aphrodite, goddess
of desire, with her young son Eros, sheltering beneath a parasol.
Unlike the first set of divinities, many of these gods did not seem to
be watching the procession at all. Indeed, Athene and Hephaestus
appeared deep in conversation. Why?

Although presented linearly, an Athenian seeing this scene for

Above While a priestess receives a footstool and the *peplos* is folded (or
unfolded), Athene converses with Hephaestus (r.). From the east side of
the Parthenon frieze. Marble relief, Athens, Greece, 438–432 BC.

the first time may have understood the gods to be sitting in a semi-circle. So, at least, it has been suggested.[140] But if, like us, the fifth-century viewer read it from left to right, he may well have realized (if our interpretation of the eastern pediment is correct) that the arrangement of the gods here on the frieze mirrored that on the pediment, outside and immediately above it. For here on the frieze were shown first the gods of the Underworld and of Eleusis and then the gods of the city, of order and of civilization, with the transition between the two groups being bridged by Hera, Zeus and Athene.

So, it is not impossible that the first viewers would have understood the sequence to suggest a journey from death to life, a sacrifice accepted, whose consequence was to be future prosperity. The significance of Eleusis and its message of hope, that from destruction comes rebirth, was foremost in the mind of an initiate.

For an Athenian who had seen his city and its temples burned, only to rise again (like the ruined olive tree which sent out its fresh shoot), the parallels would be compelling. Especially as at Salamis, only days after the burning of their city, the Athenians had struck a devastating blow against the Persian fleet, on the very day on which the Mysteries were usually performed.

Yet the gods were not the climax of the frieze. Rather, directly above the great doors which gave access to the sanctum, there were shown five human figures: two girls carrying cushioned footstools on their heads; a woman receiving one of them; and a man and a child holding up a piece of cloth. Who were these people, flanked by gods, at the very focus of the frieze? Perhaps to a fifth-century BC Athenian it was obvious. But to us, removed as we are in time and experience, there is so much about the scene which is mysterious.

Perhaps it was meant to represent the sacrifice of Erechtheus' daughter for her country. Perhaps she is the young girl with the cloth. Perhaps the other girls are her sisters and the man her father. A passage from Euripides' *Erechtheus* (first performed around 420 BC) provides a tantalizing link to the theme of heroic sacrifice resulting in great glory. Speaking at the end of the play, and describing the dead girl as one who was killed 'in defence of this country', Athene says of her and her sisters:

> They did not heedlessly abandon their oaths to their
> dear sister. So their souls have not gone down to
> Hades [i.e. the Underworld]. I have myself set them
> to live in the heavens and shall bestow on them a
> glorious name.[141]

On the other hand, it is more likely that the scene represents the presentation of the *peplos* to Athene, which formed the climax of the annual Panathenaic procession. In this case, the woman receiving the footstool is the priestess of Athene Polias (Lysimache at the time the frieze was sculpted). Her central position would certainly suggest that she is a woman of great importance. Perhaps the girls are the Arrephoroi and Ergastinai who wove the *peplos* each year for Athene. Perhaps the cloth which is being held up is the very *peplos* itself.

This is indeed most plausible. When the figures were painted, it would all have been more clear. For it is probable that painted on the sculpted cloth (just as they were woven into the real *peplos*) were scenes from the battle of the gods and giants, the very struggle which was shown just a few yards away on the east metopes. Whereas on the metopes, however, the battle was still raging, here on the frieze it was clearly over, the conflict now contained, controlled and woven into cloth to be presented to a statue of a goddess in thanks and veneration. Like the ambiguity of Hera's action – is she veiling or unveiling? – the lack of clarity about what is being done here with the cloth is probably deliberate. Is it being folded or unfolded? Is it last year's *peplos* being put away, or this year's being unpacked? The importance of the action lies in its repetition, in the continuity between one year and the next. And this was the message of Eleusis, too.

With this final scene, the strands which made up Pheidias' scheme for the sculptures of the Parthenon were woven tight together. The Persian wars, which had destroyed the unfinished temple on this same site two generations earlier, and whose struggle was mirrored in the battles of the metopes, had been weathered and won. Mirroring the birth of the goddess on the eastern pediment, Athens had been reborn. Athene and Poseidon, who had both so yearned for Attica, had both in the end protected her. And the result? The Athenians themselves, enjoying hard-won prosperity, processing in thanksgiving to the gods.

Above (from top to bottom) Casts of metopes showing the battle of the
Greeks and Amazons with, behind them, casts of the horsemen of the
frieze in situ on the Parthenon.

By 432 BC, six years after its dedication, and fifteen after it had been begun, the Parthenon was finished. It was the most perfect of all Pericles' new temples, but by now it was by no means the only one. Across Athens and Attica, ox-carts heavy with marble had been rumbling along dusty roads as the hammering of mallets clashed, cacophonous, against the clink of chisels. Sites of special sanctity or great significance had been enhanced, sites which, like us, a visitor to the next spring's drama festival, the Great Dionysia, sailing from across the seas, from Miletus or from Samos or from Ephesus, would have been eager (given time) to visit…

Part 3
The Pride
of Attica

Chapter 6

Attica Reborn

Mighty indeed are the marks and
monuments of our empire. Future
ages will wonder at us, as the present
generation wonders at us now.[142]

Above The monuments of empire: the ruins of the temple of Poseidon
at Cape Sounion. Simone Pomardi, watercolour, 1805. 66 x 104 cm.

ATHENS, SPRING 431 BC

For a delegate coming to the festival of drama at the Great
Dionysia of 431 BC, sailing in a ship west from Ionia, his first
sighting of the land of Athens, with its stony red soil and its silver
olive trees, would have been Cape Sounion. And here on the south-
east tip of Attica, perched on a high headland, its cliffs rising some
240 feet (73 metres) above the sea, stood a temple to the sea-god
Poseidon.

For many generations, it had been a place of veneration for
Athenians. Every four years, they celebrated a state festival at
Sounion, when the leading men of Athens sailed round the coast
in the state trireme to take part in solemn sacrifice,[143] and already,
when the Persians came, they were building a great limestone
temple to Poseidon. In those ghastly days of destruction, this
temple had been torched, and when the Athenians, fresh from their
victory at Salamis, returned to give thanks to the sea god, they
found nothing but blackened ruins. Here, though, to this special
place, they brought a Persian trireme, which they dragged up from
the sea and set high and dry on the headland, an offering of thanks
to Poseidon and a warning to future hostile fleets (479 BC).[144]

When rebuilding of the ruined temples could begin once more,
after the peace with Persia, Sounion was high on Perciles' list of
sites. Just as in Athens, a temple once constructed out of limestone
would be rebuilt in marble. But the somewhat brittle local marble
was less easy to work than the marble of Pentelicon. Corners were
cut. There was less fluting on the columns, and such as there was
was shallow. Yet the temple, when finished, was breathtaking – not
just in itself, but through the landscape of which it was part. And
in the temple's sanctuary, were the visitor to put into shore and
climb the steep rise to view it, could be seen a 20 feet (6 metre)
tall bronze statue of Poseidon holding the trident with which he
was once said to have struck the Acropolis in Athens. Examining

the frieze above the inner porch, the visitor may not have been surprised to find that it showed that scene so central to Athenian life, the battle of the gods and giants.[145]

Were he then to stride off some 1,300 feet (400 metres) to the north-east, the visitor would have seen a second temple. Here in a walled enclosure on a low knoll, older than the temple of Poseidon, and considerably smaller,[146] was a temple of Athene. It had been constructed in the years when Cimon exercised such power in Athens, and, like his Theseum within the city, it had not been a re-build but a new endeavour, so as such had not been subject to the Oath of Plataea (see p. 87). It was curiously asymmetrical, with Ionic pillars on two sides only, forming an L-shaped colonnade. Within it, and surrounded by a metal grille, was a massive statue of Athene, staring east towards the door and to the sunrise. The two gods who had once fought over Attica now shared this sacred place at the very limits of the land, where Poseidon's sea met Athene's earth, their protective presence recognized by any who sailed round the cape.

From Sounion, it was but a few hours' voyage west to Athens. Gradually, the coastline flattened out, and soon inland and in the distance, still far off, could be made out the city's terracotta roofs, the pale smoke drifting up from countless kilns and foundries, and above the factories and houses the Acropolis, the Parthenon glowing in the sun, the metal of its sculptures, like the spear tip of the statue of Athene Polias, glinting in the scudding light. Follow the long walls down from Athens to the sea, and he would see Piraeus laid out in its geometric grid, its low hill home to theatres and temples, its agora and harbours bustling with trade. As his ship docked in the busy port, the visitor would be struck at once by the sheer internationalism of all the boats around him and the bewildering array of goods being unpacked and unloaded on the quayside. As Pericles himself would comment the next year (430 BC):

Thanks to our city's greatness, every commodity from every land pours into Athens, so that we can enjoy products from abroad as easily as those we make or grow ourselves.[147]

A contemporary comedian, Hermippus, was more specific, listing:

ox-hides and silphium from Cyrene; mackerel and salt fish from the Bosphorus; beef ribs and pies from Thessaly ... pork and cheese from Syracuse ... salt, rope and papyrus from Egypt; frankincense from Syria; cypress-wood for [temples and statues to] the gods from Crete; plentiful ivory for sale from Libya; raisins and dried figs (to elicit pleasant dreams) from Rhodes; pears and plump apples from Euboea; slaves from Phrygia; mercenaries from Arcadia... acorns and glistening almonds from Paphlagonia; palm-fruit and fine wheat flour from Phoenicia; carpets and many-coloured pillows from Carthage.[148]

And to Piraeus too was brought the annual tribute from those states which Athens had once called her allies, and to which she now referred quite unashamedly as subjects. Early in Pericles' rise to power a decree had been passed that every state within the empire should abandon its own currency and enter into a monetary union based on Athens' drachma. Thanks to the power of its imperial economy, Athens' wealth had burgeoned. Now, each year 20,000 lbs (9,000 kg) of silver coin were shipped into Piraeus from the member states,[149] money which was paraded in the theatre before each Great Dionysia, and then stored in the strong room of the Parthenon. And each year the tribute was meticulously recorded on massive marble inscriptions on the Acropolis.

Above The temple of Hephaestus on a knoll on the north-west side of
the Agora, with the hills of Attica beyond.

From Piraeus, the visitor would walk or ride along the straight road between the towering long walls up to Athens. Because of the height of the walls, nothing could be seen on either side, only the road ahead, and the heavy traffic lumbering to and from the city. At last, the gates – some distance to the south of the Twin Tower and the Sacred Gates – and so, inside the city walls, past the small prison on the right-hand side,[150] past houses crammed tightly next to workshops, and soon into the great Agora, the public square, with its stoas and its stalls. And here, if he turned left and past the public buildings – the round State Dining Room, the Council Chamber – before you came to the Painted Stoa, the visitor would find on his left a ramp. And high on a platform on the hill above, a temple. To Hephaestus, the blacksmith god who had freed Athene from the head of Zeus.

If the temple of Hephaestus seemed curiously familiar, it was because it was almost identical to that of Poseidon at Cape Sounion. Indeed, the architect may well have been the same. Perhaps (as has been argued) it was none other than Callicrates, seconded from his duties at the Parthenon, where Ictinus now remained in sole control, to enable him to supervise a slew of temples across Attica.[151] Certainly there are similarities between many of the buildings which suggest one architect.

Set in the heart of Athens' smoke-filled metal-working district, the temple to Hephaestus had sculpted metopes at its east end only – ten on the short east side itself, depicting the labours of Heracles; and immediately round the corners to the north and south, four showing the labours of Theseus. Perhaps the other metopes were simply painted on to the smooth marble. Theseus reappeared inside the eastern porch, above the columns, on a frieze which showed him battling with a rival family for the control of Athens, while above the western porch was an old favourite: the battle of the Lapiths and centaurs. Too little of the pedimental sculptures has survived to tell with any certainty what scenes they showed, but even without them, this Hephaesteum makes a more than useful comparison with the Parthenon.

Like the Parthenon, it was constructed from Pentelic marble (though, for many of its sculptures, marble from the Cyclades was used); like the Parthenon, too, it was begun early in Pericles' building programme, perhaps around 449 BC. Yet, unlike the jewel that was the Parthenon, the Hephaesteum with its traditional proportions (six hefty columns at each shorter end and thirteen on its flanks) was in no respects exceptional, as one glance out across the Agora made clear. For looking up at the Acropolis, the comparitive superiority not only of the site itself, but of the elegance of its buildings too was obvious.

By now, the Parthenon had been joined by another stunning construction. In the days of Peisistratus, a great gateway or Propylaea had been built at the entrance to the Acropolis, at the top of the ramp leading up on to the rock. Now, in the years after the consecration of the Parthenon a new and slightly realigned Propylaea had been constructed, though not fully finished (437–432 BC). Probably the same team was employed as had worked on the Parthenon, but with Ictinus required elsewhere, they were overseen by a different architect, Mnesicles. Because it had to be built on a slope, the Propylaea had required a high level of sophistication to make it seem symmetrical to the eye. It was a triumph of design, an imposing yet harmonious complex of buildings, whose proportions blended beautifully with the Parthenon itself.

The Greeks believed that Athene had been present at the building of the Propylaea when the only recorded accident (though surely not the only accident!) had taken place:

> While the Propylaea was being constructed, there was
> a miracle, which suggested that the goddess Athene,

rather than keeping a distance, was actively assisting to complete the building work. A workman, who had been more active and hardworking than any of the rest, slipped and fell from a great height. Badly injured, he lay there for some time, and the doctors offered no hope of recovery. Pericles was very upset by the episode, but Athene came to him in a dream and recommended to him a course of treatment. When it had been applied, the man was quickly and effortlessly healed.[152]

The Propylaea did indeed appear to tower to a great height.

Above As the sun rises over the temple of Hephaestus, the Parthenon can be seen on the Acropolis (r.).

Approached from below it must have seemed as if it led not only to the Athenian Acropolis but to Mount Olympus itself. Six Doric columns (the space between the middle two enlarged to accommodate the entrance of cattle in the Panathenaic procession) supported an architrave complete with triglyphs and (blank) metopes, above which rose a pediment – intentionally mirroring the Parthenon's facade. Closer, it became apparent that within the gatehouse were more columns, and that this time (like those in the strong room of the Parthenon) they were Ionic. The coffered ceiling they supported was breathtaking in its artistry. Sculpted from white marble, it had been painted blue and studded with gold stars.

Perhaps, before walking out on to the Acropolis itself, a visitor might have taken time to turn left and enter a shaded hall, part of the Propylaea complex. This was the so-called Pinakotheke, an art gallery which sometimes doubled as state dining room. It housed a collection of paintings on wood, whose subjects in time were to include scenes from the siege of Troy.[153] But for most, the Pinakotheke could no doubt wait, for ahead, framed between the Doric pillars of the Propylaea's far facade was the towering bronze statue of Athene Promachos – and the Acropolis itself.

Even without all the buildings which were still planned for the site, the view was unrivalled anywhere. Behind Athene Promachos was the great altar at which the hundred oxen were sacrificed and burnt each year as part of the Panathenaic procession, and to the right, the Parthenon, angled perfectly to show off (for now at least)[154] its incomparable proportions. Even the light conspired to suggest that this was a sacred space, a space set apart.

For such it was. Which was why the architects had incorporated into the white marble bastion on which the Propylaea sat, a thin band of deep grey limestone. This was no mere decorative whim – rather it possessed a deeply spiritual significance. For the limestone had been quarried at Eleusis, site of the Mysteries of death and rebirth – together with the Acropolis, one of the most sacred sites in Attica. Embedded into the entrance to the Acropolis, the Eleusinian limestone formed a dynamic boundary charged with transcendental significance, through which everyone must pass, which led into another world. It was the threshold to the world of the divine.

At Eleusis itself the builders were still busy. The completion of the Parthenon had meant that craftsmen were freed to work not only on the Propylaea but on other projects, too. In 437 BC, Ictinus and his workforce travelled west along the Sacred Way. The project they were about to undertake was no less ambitious than the Parthenon and no less significant to the spiritual life of Athens. They were not only to rebuild but to enlarge the Telesterion, the great Chamber of the Mysteries at Eleusis. Here, having endured secret rites which can be but imagined, initiates would gather at the end of the great ceremony each September, safe in the knowledge that, even after physical death, life would go on. The Telesterion was planned on a quite breathtaking scale: a hall some 18,000 square feet (1,700 square metres) with the ability to accommodate 2,500 people, its vast ceiling supported by columns more than 50 feet (15 metres) in height. Around the building was to be a colonnade of thirty-two Doric columns, the same height as those which surrounded the Parthenon.[155] But because of war and economics the Telesterion would never be completed.

The role which Eleusis played in the religious life of Athens could not have been more central. It had always possessed deep spiritual significance. At its heart would always be the legendary travails of Demeter and Persephone. But after the battle of Salamis, no one could forget the part the Mysteries had played. Not only had victory coincided with the day on which the celebrations should have been performed, the *Iacchus* hymn, which had resounded inexplicably (and yet so favourably) from the dust cloud drifting from the mainland to the island and the fleet, was still sung by initiates – perhaps with greater gusto than before, as they remembered how it had presaged triumph for Athens' triremes (see p. 78). And the straits where the battle had been fought, like the beaches where the corpses of the Persian dead had been washed up, were but a stone's throw from the Telesterion.

Yet of even greater military significance was Marathon, site of the first victory against the Persians on Athenian soil. Already by the road to Marathon, in the foothills of Hymettus and Pentelicon, another temple had been built. On the same model as the Hephaesteum in Athens and the temple of Poseidon at Cape Sounion, this temple to Athene stood roughly halfway on the route Miltiades and his exhausted men had marched after they had fought the Persians, and as they hurried back to Phalerum where they feared the enemy might beach. Of the temple nothing now survives. It was later dismantled to be rebuilt in the Agora at Athens where it was dedicated to Ares, god of war, in the reign of the Roman emperor Augustus.[156]

Nearer to Marathon more building work had taken place. On a low rise to the north of the battlefield, overlooking to the east the undulating island of Euboea and the sea, and to the south the long plain and the battlefield bounded by the hills of Attica, was the sanctuary at Rhamnous, where one of the most terrifying goddesses of all was worshipped: Nemesis, goddess of revenge and retribution.

Legend told how to escape from the desire of Zeus, Nemesis had turned herself into a swan. But Zeus transformed himself as well, and the two divine swans scudded low across the sea, to the rhythmic beating of their wings, until they came to Rhamnous. Here, exhausted, Nemesis fell to earth, and here Zeus raped her. In time, she gave birth to a child, hatched from a swan's egg. The child was Helen, like Pandora the most beautiful of evils, and the

cause not only of the Trojan War but of lasting hatred between
Greece and Persia.[157] Perhaps the Persians had heard the story too.
When they came to Greece they were said to have been

> so convinced that nothing would prevent them from
> over-running Athens that they shipped with them a
> block of marble from the island of Paros, to raise a
> trophy to commemorate their deeds.[158]

But their hopes were dashed at Marathon. In the aftermath of their
retreat, the marble block was found abandoned on the battlefield.
How deliciously appropriate it was, now, when the temples were
again being raised, that here at Rhamnous, a sanctuary dedicated
to Revenge, this very block should be its temple's centrepiece; how
redolent of vengeance that the raw marble from which the Persians
had meant to make their trophy should now be shaped into the
head of Nemesis. Later wrongly believed to have been sculpted
by Pheidias himself, the statue was by his pupil Agoracritus. It was
housed in a new temple, whose style suggests that it was built by
the same architect – or team – as built the temples of Hephaestus
in the Agora and of Poseidon at Sounion, and whose first stone
may have been laid at the solemn Festival of Nemesis in late
September 436 BC.[159]

  According to the traveller Pausanias the statue wore

> on its head a crown decorated with deer and
> miniature Victories ... On its plinth is shown Helen
> being brought from Nemesis to Leda's breast.[160]

The birth of Helen, shown here on the base of the statue of
Nemesis at Rhamnous parallels the creation of Pandora on the
plinth of the Pheidias' Athene in the Parthenon. Both sculptures

showed the coming into the world of a beautiful woman who would sow destruction: Pandora, crafted by the gods; Helen born from the seed of Zeus. Both women were the cause of misery. Pandora had spawned universal suffering; Helen had sparked the legendary Trojan War. With their invasion, Troy's heirs, the Persians, had provoked a second Trojan War, fought this time on the soil of Greece, but again the Greeks had won. From her shrine at Rhamnous, Nemesis had reaped grim retribution and through the agency of the Athenians, whose dead still lay beneath their grave mound on the haunted plain

Above A memorial to hubris, this fragment is all that remains from the head of Nemesis carved from a marble block abandoned by the Persians at Marathon. Attica, Greece, 430–420 BC.

of Marathon, the Persians had been defeated.

The marble block abandoned by the blood-streaked shore at Marathon was not the only relic of a battlefield to stir the inspiration of the Athenians. At Plataea, that last great conflict of the Persian Wars to be fought in mainland Greece, the victors had found a tent, which they believed belonged to the Great King Xerxes himself (see Chapter 3). The fate of the tent itself is hotly disputed,[161] but it may have inspired one of the most remarkable of all the buildings of Pericles' ambitious programme: the so-called Odeon which sprawled beneath the southern face of the Acropolis, beside the Theatre of Dionysus, a covered hall in which took place the contests for musicians, now elevated to become a major part of the Panathenaic Games.

Before his ostracism, Themistocles was said to have constructed an Odeon here, built partly from the masts and yard arms of the Persian triremes captured or disabled at Salamis.[162] Now, Pericles had gone one better. Perhaps reusing much of the woodwork, imbued as it was with such patriotic symbolism, Pericles commissioned on the site a vast building. Sitting proudly on a terrace 28 feet (8.5 metres) high, the Odeon was around 200 feet (60 metres) square, with a roof rising to a central apex 65 feet (20 metres) tall, the whole surrounded by a colonnade.[163] What made the building so special was not just its huge size or the sheer architectural skill which had gone into its creation. Rather,

> with its interior arranged to accommodate many rows
> of seats and columns, and its circular roof sloping from
> a central apex, it was said to be an exact replica of the
> Great King Xerxes' tent ... At the same time, striving
> for renown, Pericles had a law passed that a music
> competition be added to the Panathenaic Festival. He
> himself was elected one of the judges and laid down the

rules for how contestants should sing or perform on the *aulos* or lyre. From then on, audiences came to the Odeon to hear these musical competitions.[164]

With its infrastructure of Persian masts from Salamis and its design inspired by the Persian tent captured at Plataea, both integrated now into a building dedicated not to war but to the arts of peace, the Odeon was the physical embodiment of the image that Athenians wished to present of how their fortunes had been transformed over the past fifty years (479–431 BC).

Yet now, in the spring of 431 BC, the world was about to change once more. The years of Pericles' supremacy had brought prosperity to his own city, but to Athens' rivals his imperial expansionist policies were being viewed with increasing suspicion. With the Athenian empire now effectively an Aegean superpower, independent cities like Corinth, whose wealth was built on foreign trade, were becoming seriously worried. Especially when Athens imposed an economic embargo on Megara, now a so-called hostile city state, preventing it from doing business within her empire. As the months went by it became clearer that war between the Greek states loomed just beyond the horizon.

This was the atmosphere which permeated Athens as visitors from across her empire gathered to participate in the theatre nestling beside the Odeon and below the cliffs of the Acropolis for the festival of drama at the Great Dionysia. After the tribute from the subject states had been paraded on the stage and after the sons of that year's war dead, killed in skirmishes beyond the borders, had been honoured, the three-day festival of drama could begin. This year it included a play by Euripides and it was intended to provoke.

Medea told the story of an eastern princess (from a land now part of Persia) brought back to Greece by Jason, when (like a fifth-century Athenian plying his way back to Piraeus from the Black Sea, his ship laden with grain) he returned from his successful quest to find the golden fleece. But Jason was exiled and the couple found themselves in Corinth, where Jason abandoned Medea to marry the king's young daughter. Distraught, Medea plotted retribution. But, as the drama showed, she would have been unable to succeed in her revenge had not Aegeus, king of Athens, unexpectedly arrived to offer her asylum. Buoyed up by her encounter, Medea wreaked a terrible punishment on Jason, killing their sons and refusing even to let him bury them. Hidden just below the surface of Euripides' play there seemed to be a threat. By blindly offering to harbour Medea once she had declared war on Athens' (contemporary) enemy Corinth, Aegeus, the embodiment of Athens, had admitted into his city a destructive force, the consequences of which he could not begin to imagine. In the subsequent myth, with which the audience was familiar, Medea would seduce Aegeus and try, albeit unsuccessfully, to kill his son. And Aegeus' son was none other than the great Athenian hero Theseus himself.

Be careful, Euripides was warning the Athenians. Like Pandora and Helen, Medea was a 'beautiful evil'. While war with Corinth might seem attractive, it could in the end bring destruction. In the play, immediately after Aegeus had departed. there was a choral song for which Euripides had written lyrics. Not only did they encapsulate the patriotic pride of Athens and the Athenians' belief in their special relationship with the gods, now celebrated in new temples throughout Attica, they told too of Euripides' fear for the future:

> Since time began, the citizens of Athens have been
> rich indeed, the children of Erechtheus, the children
> of the blessed gods, the dwellers in a holy land that's
> whole and pure. And so they grew strong in the
> shining light of wisdom, stepping lightly in the clear
> pellucid air, where once they say that golden-headed

Harmony gave birth to the nine sacred Muses – and
the clear-flowing waters of Cephisus nurtures them.

They say that Aphrodite, goddess of desire, drinks
deep of the Cephisus, sailing in her barge to Athens,
fanned by breezes scented in the honeyed air; and,
on her hair, her retinue of lusts which bring sweet
knowledge (so beguiling) in their train, scatter flowers,
seductive in the soothing scent of garlands twined with
blushing damask rose.

And so I ask: how will the city welcome you, Medea?
How will Cephisus with his sacred streams, how will
the very soil of Athens learn to love you, stained
by the blood-guilt of your sacrilege, your own sons'
murderess?[165]

Almost exactly two centuries before, in the wake of Cylon's coup
d'etat, the Alcmaeonidae had been expelled from Athens lest their
bloodguilt pollute and so destroy the city. Now, through his use of
the Medea myth, Euripides was warning that a new destructive
force might be unleashed on Attica. And, just as Aegeus could not
foresee the consequences of harbouring Medea, so Athens now
could not predict the outcome of the coming war.

As the choral song resounded in the theatre below, high up on
the Acropolis, in the shallow pool which had been built beneath the
statue of Athene in the Parthenon to prevent its ivory from drying
out, there was reflected in the placid waters Pheidias' Athene, her
arm outstretched, her hand supporting a winged Victory. Yet the
statue was gazing east, to Persia, while in the west, from Corinth,
diplomats were already fanning out to allied states, to Thebes and
Sparta, to discuss terms for a war coalition against Athens.

War was inevitable, and in just two years the orchards and vineyards and the olive groves of Attica, the 'holy land' that was so 'whole and pure', would be scorched in fire, and the very temples, built as symbols of self-certainty and pride, would be choked with the rotting corpses of Athenian dead.[166]

Above The realities of war: a hoplite (stylized and naked) defends a comrade, fallen in battle. Red-figure cup, Attica, Greece, c.420 BC. H. 11.4 cm.

Chapter 7

Death of a Dream

*One's sense of honour is the only thing
that does not grow old.*[167]

Like a trireme captain deliberately steering his ship into stormy
waves, Pericles had set his city on a calculated course for war with
Sparta and her allies. To establish the power of Athens' empire once
and for all was his intention, and if this meant a short-term sacrifice,
it would be worth it. Such sacrifice was after all in Athens' blood.
In a few years, he argued, it would all be over. Athens would have
taught her rivals a lesson they would not forget.

For almost thirty years, Pericles had held sway in Athens. An
entire generation had grown up under his leadership. Yet, even so,
the policy he now proposed met with serious opposition. Unlike her
land army, Athens' navy was unbeatable, so it was Pericles' strategy
to concentrate entirely on winning victory by sea. This meant not
only conducting coastal raids on enemy territory, but to all intents
and purposes abandoning entirely the countryside of Attica itself
to hostile raids and relying on a constant flow of food shipped in
to Piraeus from abroad and transported to the city through the
protected corridor of the Long Walls. It meant turning Athens into
a landlocked island.

For much of Athens' population this was shocking. It was not
only the aristocrats with their vast country estates who stood to

suffer. Many of the city residents owned plots of land outside the city walls, while for most country dwellers the land was their only livelihood. Not only that – surely the countryside of Attica was, in the words of the chorus they had heard just weeks before, 'a holy land that's whole and pure', fought over by the gods themselves, sacred to their protectress Athene. Still, the Assembly voted to back Pericles.

Soon Attica's sheep and cattle were being ferried across the strait near Rhamnous to Euboea, while the roads leading into the city became clogged with country folk: men driving jolting ox-carts on which elderly relations, many weeping, sat among possessions piled precariously high, veiled women clutching cages crammed with squawking hens, yelping dogs and children getting mixed up in the general melee. They had left behind them nothing which could be moved or used by an invading army. Even the doors and window frames of houses were removed. With grim foreboding hanging heavy in the dusty air, the sea of refugees poured through the city gates and on into every vacant plot in Athens as temporary encampments were pitched within the Agora, or by the road which ran between the Long Walls, even within the sanctuaries of the gods themselves. And so, close packed together, they hunkered down and waited.

Less than a month after the performance of *Medea* at the Great Dionysia of 431 BC, Plataea, Athens' one ally at Marathon, had fallen to the enemy. Now, news came that Eleusis, too, was taken, and the corn fields all around had been destroyed. The enemy forces were moving closer. They had passed Aegaleus. They had made camp at Acharnae, just 7 miles (11 km) from Athens. And still Pericles forbade the army to go out and fight. As the faint stench of smoke from blazing homesteads drifted into Athens, the feeling of outrage grew. To the elderly it was a harsh reminder of what they had endured once, when the Persians came; to the young, confident in their belief of Athens' god-given invincibility, it was inexplicable. Yet still Pericles succeeded in imposing his will. The Athenian navy, sailing round the Peloponnese, was doing equal damage to the enemy and, when at last the invading army did withdraw from Attica, Pericles chose his moment. He led the Athenian army, around 16,000 young men hungry for revenge,[168] out through the blackened countryside to vent their pent-up anger against Megara. As they marched, victorious, back to Athens, the army would have met the country folk of Attica returning to their devastated homes, their crops burned, their trees cut down, their vineyards uprooted and their livelihoods destroyed, many undoubtedly questioning the strategy that Pericles had imposed upon them.

Yet, come the end of winter, it was Pericles they chose to make the customary speech at the Demosion Sema, the public burial ground, in honour of the war dead (430 BC), the speech in which, at least according to Thucydides, he encapsulated his soaring vision of Athens' greatness. Among the tombstones by the road to the Academy, his words ringing clearly in the early dawn, he sought to remind the citizens of all that they were fighting for: freedom of speech and freedom of action, a freedom dependent on civic courage which in turn gave rise to civic content. 'Where the rewards for courage are the greatest,' he concluded, 'there you will find citizens imbued with the best and most courageous spirits.'

For the moment, it seemed that Pericles' strategy was holding. As springtime came to Attica, so the almost endless stream of refugees swarmed back through the city gates, and the swollen population settled down to endure another season, watching as their fields and farms were once more occupied and ruined. Yet nothing could prepare them for what that year would bring.

A plague had broken out in upper Egypt. From there it had spread rapidly to Libya and Persia, and soon it had reached the coastal cities with which Athens traded and on which her citizens relied (now more than ever) for supplies. Now the bacterium was on board the merchant ships, and making for Piraeus. It came ashore first in Piraeus, then raced up through the Long Walls and into the overcrowded city itself. Its effects were devastating: first, inflammation of the eyes; then bleeding tongues and throats; and rasping breath; then sneezing, coughing, vomiting and fever; ulcers; suppurating pustules; uncontrollable diarrhoea; paralysis of fingers, genitals and toes; amnesia; and almost certain death. As Thucydides, who, remarkably, recovered from the plague, records:

> The fact that country dwellers had been moved into the city made things much worse … In the heat of summer, they were living not in houses but in poorly ventilated huts, and so they died like flies. The bodies of the dying were piled on top of one another; the half-dead could be seen stumbling along streets or massing around fountains in their search of water.[169]

Even more tellingly, given the great building programme which had galvanized Attica in the years immediately before,

> the temples, in which many were living, were piled high with the corpses of those who had died inside. It was such a humanitarian disaster that people started to ignore every law, both religious and civic, since they had no idea what would happen next. Funeral rites were in disarray. Many people … without the means for proper burial, because their families had been devastated by so many deaths, resorted to desperate means. They would stumble across pyres, already built in preparation by another family, lay their own dead on them and light them before the others could arrive

– or, they would find a blazing pyre and throw the
corpse that they were carrying on top of it and then
run off.

Nor were these the only effects upon public morality and religion:

> Prayers offered in temples, consultation of oracles and
> the rest were all equally useless. Eventually, people
> were so overwhelmed by suffering that they no longer
> paid these things any attention ... It seemed the same
> whether a man worshipped the gods or not, when
> you could see the pious and the bad dying quite at
> random.

As the months dragged on and no end seemed in sight, the whole
edifice of Periclean Athens seemed set to crumble from its fragile
facade inwards to its core, as one by one the values praised so
enthusiastically in the stirring speech made at the public cemetery
evaporated in the oily smoke of choking pyres throughout the dying
city. In the end, the disease took hold of Pericles himself (429 BC).
Once he had prided himself on his rationality; now, as he felt the
plague take hold of him, he resorted to amulets and lucky charms.
As Pericles lay dying, his fiercely intellectual mind began to wander.
The group of loyal friends who had gathered by his bedside might
try to find a reasoned explanation for his last whispered words, that
'no Athenian ever put on mourning because of me'; but they were
nothing but febrile ravings.

At its peak, the policies of Pericles had made Athens rich,
as the city's fortunes, battered in the Persian Wars, had been
transformed. The speech that Pericles had made on a cold winter's
dawn in 430 BC had encapsulated in inspiring rhetoric everything
he had achieved, just as the Parthenon had embodied it in marble.

But perhaps it had contained not a small element of hubris, that supreme confidence in one's success that in Greek thought was certain to attract the anger of the gods. And punishment. For, it was thanks to Pericles that Attica was being burned once more, and that its citizens were dying in droves throughout its temples and its streets, and that the very values which he had sought so hard to instil in his people's hearts and minds were being rejected.

Pericles' death left a vacuum in the life of Athens. Its citizenry, unused to real political plurality, now found itself wooed by seductive demagogues. In the years that followed, as the plague abated leaving a third of the population (and fighting force) of Athens dead, Pericles' military strategy was gradually abandoned. After ten years of heavy losses and an ever-spiralling descent into brutality, the war was terminated by the signing of the Peace of Nicias, thanks to whose terms little had been achieved on either side (421 BC).

In Athens, perhaps to re-establish a sense of civic unity and pride, peace gave the politicians an excuse to revisit not only some of the ideals which seemed to have died with Pericles, but his construction programme too. On the Acropolis, there still remained one crucial temple which had never been rebuilt, perhaps the most important and iconic of them all. So, the war with the Peloponnese now over, and almost sixty years since its predecessor had been burnt by the Persians, work began at last on the temple of Athene Polias, which, although it was newer than the Parthenon would soon be known in Athens as 'the most venerable'.

Unlike the Parthenon, which had been raised on the site of the ruined temple started after Marathon but left incomplete when Xerxes' army had destroyed it, the new temple of Athene Polias would not be constructed on the foundations of its predecessor but slightly to the north. Because of the sloping terrain and the many functions which it was intended to perform, the building would take on a curiously hybrid form, not so much one temple but a temple complex.[170] Both of the original gifts offered by Athene and Poseidon in their contest for the land of Attica would be housed within its bounds: the olive tree and the salt water well, complete with the marks of the god's trident at its mouth.

Just as the Parthenon frieze showed worshippers processing in honour not only of Athene but of all the gods, so in the new temple of Athene Polias many deities would be revered. When it was finished in 404 BC, the complex incorporated shrines to at least ten gods and heroes associated with the early history of Athens, not least the tomb of Cecrops and the pit in which Erichthonius, the snake, was housed.

At the east end, beyond a pedimented porch supported on six slender Ionic columns, their capitals sparkling with coloured glass beads set into their moulding, a great door opened into a chamber in which, at last, was housed the most sacred of all the city's statues: the ancient olive-wood image of Athene. Positioned so as to face the great sacrificial altar and the dawn, this holiest of likenesses was kept constantly lit by the light of a golden lamp, the craftsmanship of the sculptor Callimachus. Pausanias, the traveller, wrote of how

> they fill the lamp with oil on the same day every year –
> and all that time, there is enough oil to feed the lamp,
> although it shines perpetually both night and day. The
> wick is made from flax from the Carpas Peninsula [in
> Cyprus], the only variety which fire will not consume.
> Above the lamp is a bronze palm-tree which ascends
> to the roof and draws up the smoke.[171]

Pausanias also saw an ancient wooden statue of Hermes, which (his guides assured him) had originally been dedicated by Cecrops, and a number of dedications to Athene. Among them were two items of especial resonance,

the breast-plate of Masistius, the Persian cavalry
commander at Plataea, and a Persian sword said to
have belonged to [the general] Mardonius.[172]

The ghosts of the Persian Wars were still not forgotten. The
Parthenon had housed their memories; now the temple of Athene
Polias did, too.

To move round to the north required Pausanias to descend a
series of some eleven or twelve steps, as the level of the ground here
was 10 feet (3 metres) lower than at the east. Here, surprisingly, he
would have found another porch, fronted by four towering columns,
with another on each side, leading in to yet another sanctuary.
Unusually, in the south-east corner of the porch, the builders had
left an opening in the roof, directly above a small recess which

Above The temple of Athene Polias (now known as the Erechtheum). The
'Caryatid Porch' was deliberately built over the ruins of the earlier temple
burned by Xerxes.

was set into the paving, and in turn was framed by an altar. It marked a place of indescribable holiness: the very spot where Zeus' thunderbolt had smashed against the rock as the god intervened to put an end to the quarrel between Poseidon and Athene, the very moment, in fact, shown on the Parthenon's western pediment, when Attica was awarded to Athene.[173] Pausanias sadly made no mention of it, but he did record that

> as you enter, there are altars to Poseidon (where they make sacrifices to Erechtheus, too, in obedience to an oracle) as well as of the hero Boutes and of Hephaestus … It is a double building, and inside it there is sea-water in a well … Remarkably, when the wind blows to the south, the sound of waves issues from the well. The mark of the trident is on the rock.[174]

On his right, as he entered the sanctuary, was another, smaller door, leading out (somewhat surprisingly) into a garden. This was the Garden of Pandrosus, the only one of Cecrops' three daughters who had obeyed Athene's orders not to open the casket in which the baby Erichthonius had been concealed (see p. 30). Here in a walled enclosure next to a free-standing shrine was another totem, redolent with mystery: Athene's sacred olive tree, offered as her pledge to Athens, burnt to its roots by the Persians, only to sprout a new shoot the next day.

From the Garden of Pandrosus, on the southern side, another flight of steps led up and out on to the foundations of the ruined ancient temple of Athene Polias, all that remained of Hippias' great building. Perhaps because it was so venerated, this site would be left bare. Nothing would be built on it – except, that is, for one porch jutting out from the south side of the new temple. The porch itself was divided into two zones. A high wall running continuously around

the three external faces was surmounted not by columns but by six
sculpted female figures, each seven feet 6 inches (2.3 metres) tall, the
marble pillows on whose heads supported a flat roof. Known in the
fifth century BC simply as the 'maidens' (*Korai*),[175] these sculptures
in the round were mirrors of the girls on the east frieze of the
Parthenon. Like them, they showed well-born Athenians, their ankle-
length dresses gathered gracefully in folds, their heads held high, their
abundant hair cascading down their backs. Like the girls of the frieze
they carried shallow bowls from which to pour libations to the gods.

The purpose of the porch remains uncertain. Perhaps the woven
peplos of Athene was displayed here, with its scenes of gods and
giants. But whatever its use, it was stunning. Undoubtedly the statues
of the girls were painted, their faces (like the cheeks of Pheidias'
Athene) rubbed pink, their lips red, their eyes staring out across the
ruins of the ancient temple to the Parthenon. Their vitality was
quite intentional. Near them, deliberately placed to magnify the
contrast, could be seen

> some ancient statues of Athene, not completely
> destroyed, but blackened and too fragile to withstand
> injury. They were burnt when the Athenians withdrew
> to their ships and the Persian King captured the city,
> now it had been abandoned by its young men.[176]

Like the Propylaea, the temple of Athene Polias contained a seam
of dark limestone from Eleusis, just over 2 feet (0.65 metres) high,
running round the outside of the building on the band above the
columns. Onto this, unusually, were affixed figures carved in white
marble, showing warriors and horses, chariots and women. But what
the frieze depicted, we do not know. No record has survived, and the
figures we still have are quite ambiguous.

Ambiguity also surrounds the last of the temples that was built on

the Acropolis in the fifth century BC, and which may (like the temple
of Athene Polias) have been originally conceived as part of Pericles'
great programme. High on a bastion jutting out to the south of the
Propylaea, its walls refaced and dressed in the years before Peisistratus
was tyrant, was built a temple to Athene Nike (Athene, Goddess of
Victory). The date of its construction is debated, but perhaps it was
already under way when war with the Peloponnesians broke out in
431 BC. Certainly, its building had already been decreed long before,
when the Parthenon was first begun – and its architect had been
assigned, too: Callicrates, one of the two architects of the Parthenon.
Perhaps progress had been interrupted by the onset of the war, and
by the plague. At any rate, it seems that it was not until peace was
restored in 421 BC that work on the temple could continue.

In its design it was elegant, feminine and almost fragile – especially
when compared to the towering masculinity of the Propylaea which
it flanked. Built of Pentelic marble, it was tiny – a mere 18 by 27 feet
(5.4 by 8.17 metres) at its base, with two porches, one to the east,
the other to the west, each with pediments supported by four Ionic
columns; and it contained just one room, open to the east. At some
stage, perhaps after the signing of the Peace of Nicias (421 BC), the

Above Greeks fight fellow Greeks on the temple of Athene Nike's chilling
frieze. Marble relief. Athens, Greece, c.425 BC. H. 44.5 cm.

temple was adorned with sculptures. Above each of the corners of the pediments, bronze Victories stretched flashing wings, while on the western pediment (it seems) the battle of the Greeks and Amazons was shown, clearly visible from the Hill of Ares on which, according to mythology, those warrior women had once camped. And on the east? The battle of the gods and giants, the conflict which more than any other tied the sculptures of the Acropolis not only to each other but to the religious life of Athens itself.

Below this eastern pediment, on the frieze which ran around the architrave, the gods were shown again, this time at peace. It was a scene of birth which mirrored that on the base of Pheidias' great statue of Athene Parthenos. But whereas that showed the birth of Pandora, here it was the birth of Athene herself – the episode shown with such vigour on the Parthenon's eastern pediment. Here on the Victory temple, though, all seemed more relaxed, as if Athene's birth (and by association Athens' greatness) was no longer a miracle but a cosmic certainty.

On the temple's three other sides, battle scenes adorned the frieze. Executed maybe in the years of peace, they departed from the now familiar themes. No centaurs here, or Amazons. Rather, the combatants were all from the real world. To the south, Greeks were fighting against Persians, immediately recognizable by their costumes and their armour. Perhaps inspired by the depiction of the battle in the Painted Stoa, these may have been the first temple sculptures on the Acropolis to show the victory at Marathon, a victory whose impact had pervaded the whole building project.

But even more telling – and more chilling, too – were the subjects of the two remaining sides. To the north and west, the frieze showed battles in which Greeks fought Greeks. Which battles they were meant to represent, we do not know. It does not really matter. What matters is that here at the entrance to the Acropolis, the buildings of which had been inspired by the victory (as their creators would have had it) of Greek civilization over barbaric foreigners, the narrative had suddenly been changed. The focus had been narrowed. No longer were order and enlightenment the preserve of Greeks *as Greeks*. Now, there was a hierarchy. Now, the frieze appeared to say, the beacon of civilization belonged to Athens. Her Greek enemies, just as the Persians had once been, were no more than barbarians. And, as such, they must be conquered. It was perhaps the logical conclusion to Pericles' speech, yet it heralded a new age, an age recorded with grim observation by Thucydides.

In the years after the Peace of Nicias, Athens continued to flex her muscles. In 416 BC, her fleet sailed into the harbour of the tiny island of Melos. The Melians had remained neutral during Athens' war with Sparta, but now Athens insisted that they join her side. So startling were the arguments which the Athenian negotiators used to persuade the islanders, that Thucydides (in a passage unique in all his writings) chose to dramatize it, recreating albeit imaginatively the dialogue between the two sides. Almost immediately, the Athenians go straight to the heart of the matter:

> We will employ no extravagant arguments – for example, that we have a right to empire because we defeated the Persians ... Rather, this is our advice: try to get everything you can, based on hard reality. We both know that when things are discussed by sensible people, justice depends on having enough power to enforce it. In fact, the strong do what they have the power to do, and the weak have to accept it.[177]

This is the new world order epitomized on the deceptively elegant facade of the temple of Athene Nike, a world in which comedians could mock surviving veterans of the Persian Wars and Marathon (albeit now in their late eighties and nineties) for being out of touch,

for belonging to another age.[178] On Melos, Athens' new justice was soon meted out. The city was sacked, its menfolk slaughtered, its women and children led off in chains to slavery.

In 415 BC, buoyed by a belief in their invincibility, the Athenians launched a massive armada against the grain-rich island of Sicily. One of its three generals was the egotistical young Alcibiades. Almost since birth he had lived with Pericles as his adopted son, but in his flamboyant arrogance he was Pericles' polar opposite. Even before the expedition could set out, an event occurred in

Above The deceptively elegant temple of Athene Nike rises from its buttress beside the Propylaea (l.).

Athens which shook the city to its core. One night, the statues of Hermes which stood not only in the Agora but in front of almost every house to protect its occupants and to avert the evil eye, were smashed – an act not only of wanton vandalism but of calculated impiety and ill omen. The fleet was allowed to sail, but Alcibiades was soon recalled, charged by his enemies not only with this sacrilege but with blasphemy. He had, they claimed, parodied the sacred Mysteries of Eleusis, revealing their hidden secrets to an uninitiated slave. No matter whether he was guilty. It was the sort of thing the citizens could well imagine than an Alcmaeonid, and Alcibiades in particular, would do, and it carried the death penalty.

When they tried to arrest him, Alcibiades fled – first to Sparta, with which Athens was once more at war. Here, he gave his city's enemy devastatingly useful military secrets, but when even the Spartans realized that he was a destabilizing force, Alcibiades was compelled to flee again. This time his choice of sanctuary was even more outrageous. Like Themistocles before him – or the tyrant Hippias – he turned for refuge to the ancient enemy not only of his city but of Greece. He fled to Persia. And in an act of treachery to make the plain of Marathon resound all the more monstrously to the groans of the ghostly dead, he once more traded defence intelligence for his life.

Yet, remarkably, in 411 BC, in the wake of the disastrous defeat of the Athenian expedition to Sicily and a series of military setbacks, Alcibiades was recalled to Athens. Ironically, when he eventually returned to Piraeus from campaign (407 BC), it was on the day when, every year, the ancient olive statue of Athene was removed from the Acropolis and taken to be ritually washed by immersion in the sea. For the Athenians it was a day of ill omen. The goddess, after all, was no longer in the city. Athens was vulnerable. And so it was that Alcibiades returned to an unguarded Athens, and to the supreme command.

For five years (411–406 BC), Alcibiades led Athens' troops to victory – and it is to this period that the last of the Acropolis' fifth-century BC sculptures have been attributed: a marble parapet, which ran, some 3 feet (1 metre) high and 100 feet (30 metres) in total length, above the jutting lip of the bastion on which the temple of Athene Nike had been built.

In some of the most exquisite artwork of its age, it showed Athene, goddess of victory, seated on a rock. Around her were winged Victories, some adorning trophies with the armour of defeated Persians or hoplite Greeks or with equipment seized from captured ships, while others led sleek cattle to be sacrificed. The artistry was breathtaking, perhaps a final blossoming of the work of the men who had created not only the sculptures on the Parthenon, but on the temple of Athene Polias and all those other temples across Attica as well.

But even as these Victories were being set in place, the seeds of Athens' ruin were already germinating. In the wake of a defeat at sea near Ephesus, Alcibiades, always suspect, was exiled once more. As Athens was faced with financial ruin, the gold statues were removed from the Acropolis and melted down as coinage. As the final touches were being made to the temple of Athene Polias, ready to receive Athene's ancient statue, an Athenian fleet sailed for the Bosphorus, to do battle with the enemy. But, despite a last attempt by Alcibiades to intervene to save it, Athens' navy was defeated. Some 3,000 of her men were captured. All were killed. Within weeks the Spartans were blockading the harbours at Piraeus. Athens was under siege.

In those last days of summer (404 BC), the citizens of Athens, trapped now and impotent, still saw the sun rise every dawn to bathe the Acropolis in light. The bridles of the horses on the Parthenon's eastern pediment still shimmered in the daybreak; the spear tip of Pheidias' bronze statue of Athene Promachos still flashed; the outstretched wings of the Victories on the temple of Athene Nike still glittered triumphantly. But in the city itself there was no one who did not know that defeat was now inevitable. Perhaps Athens would suffer the fate which she herself had inflicted upon Melos only twelve years earlier. Yet, as husbands and fathers contemplated their own deaths and the enslavement of their womenfolk, the peace terms were read out. The people of Athens would be spared. Only its city walls and the Long Walls leading to the sea would be dismantled. In victory, despite the patriotic words of Pericles in his speech for the dead a generation earlier, Sparta and her allies had shown themselves more magnanimous by far than Athens. In the end, Athens had believed her own propaganda and, thinking herself invincible, had been defeated.

Opposite A winged Victory adjusts her sandal on the balustrade of the temple of Athene Nike. Marble, Athens, Greece, c.425 BC.

Epilogue

In the century after Athens' defeat in the Peloponnesian War, the Greek world changed unrecognizably. So did its relationship with Persia. In fact, even in the desperate second phase of the war, the two sides (Athens and her empire; Sparta and her allies) had been trying with increasing success to curry favour with their one-time Persian enemies. So Sparta's victory was funded by Persian gold. A precedent

had been set and, with the implosion of Athens' empire making Greece increasingly unstable, more and more Greek cities found themselves financing wars with the help of Persia. Even the Athenians swallowed their pride and went a begging.

Given this new political reality, and as the battles of Marathon and Salamis faded into distant memories, the themes of the Parthenon's sculptures lost their immediacy and relevance, and instead their allegories of civilized Athens triumphing over barbarian Persia may even have become embarrassing reminders of how much things had

changed. Then, just sixty-six years after Athens fell to Sparta, there was another seismic shift. An army marched south from Macedonia, joined battle with a combined force of Athenians and Thebans at Chaironeia (338 BC) and defeated them. Within weeks the rest of Greece surrendered.

Those who believed in omens might have known that Macedonia would topple the old order. The sign had been all too clear. For on the day the Macedonian king heard of his son's birth, he heard too that one of the most beautiful temples in the Greek world had been destroyed. The temple was the Artemision at Ephesus, deliberately torched by an arsonist called Herostratus, so that his name would enter history. And the king's son? Alexander, who would be called the Great.

Alexander entered Athens in triumph. Undoubtedly he saw the sights and understood the meaning of the Parthenon, for only four years later (May 334 BC) Alexander led an army against Persia. Once across the Dardanelles, he stopped at Troy. Here he sacrificed to Athene and poured a libation to the Trojan heroes. Days later he defeated the Persians at the river Granicus, and from the spoils he sent fourteen Persian shields as trophies back to Athens to be affixed onto the east facade of the Parthenon.[179]

Years later, Alexander would propose to build a temple of Athene on the acropolis of Troy itself, but he died before it could be started (323 BC). So it was left to later dynasts to undertake the work and, when they did, they used it to make a quite remarkable statement. For the new temple's metopes showed not just the legendary sack of Troy but three other battles: those between the gods and giants, the Lapiths and the centaurs and the Greeks and Amazons. Their subject matter had been deliberately chosen to be identical to those of the Parthenon. Here at Troy, on the eve of his invasion, Xerxes had vowed to avenge the city's defeat at the hands of Greeks. Yet he himself had been defeated and the Parthenon erected in remembrance. Now the message of the Parthenon had been brought back to Troy itself. The story had gone full circle.

In the following centuries, Athens' status remained high. A long history as the intellectual capital of Greece meant that the city now became a thriving university town, while visitors flocked to admire its architectural treasures. On the Acropolis, as well as on the steps of the Parthenon itself, forests of new statues sprang up, including two massive square pillars, one by the ramp in front of the Pinakotheke, the other hard by the south-east corner of the Parthenon. Each was topped by a gleaming four-horse chariot dedicated by King Eumenes II of Pergamum to mark his victory in the Panathenaic Games (178 BC).

Then in 146 BC, Rome turned its sights on Greece. Corinth was sacked, its treasures looted, and the legions marched on Athens. In the dying days of the Roman Republic, Athens' lure was such that the philhellene Mark Antony spent long months there with Cleopatra.[180] But it was Antony's nemesis, the first Roman emperor Augustus (ruled 31 BC–AD 15), ever one to boost his profile, who ordered the erection of a delicate round building facing the east side of the Parthenon. It was an Ionic temple dedicated to Rome and to Augustus himself, a none too subtle marker that the Acropolis at last had a new master.

Augustus was not alone in making his egotistical mark on the Acropolis and wider Attica. Where Alexander's shields had once been displayed on the east facade of the Parthenon, Nero fixed a bronze inscription in his own honour. But other emperors were more sensitive. In the reign of Marcus Aurelius (AD 161–80) a new monumental gateway was constructed at the entrance to the sanctuary at Eleusis. Built in Pentelic marble, it was modelled on the Propylaea of the Athenian Acropolis, whose bastion had incorporated a thin band of grey Eleusinian limestone. So now the entrances to the Acropolis and to the Eleusinian sanctuary were identical, the clearest evidence that in the mindset of antiquity the two sites were inextricably bound together.

Soon Greece would be in turmoil once again. In AD 267, the Heruli, Gothic tribesmen, fought their way inside the walls of Athens. Terrified, the citizens took refuge on the Acropolis and so escaped destruction.

Previous pages The Parthenon as a romantic ruin looking west towards the setting sun. James Skene, graphite, pen and ink, and watercolour, 1838–43. 32.2 x 57.3 cm.

But it was faith, not violence which wreaked the greatest havoc on the Parthenon and the Acropolis. Between AD 389 and 391 the Christian Roman emperor Theodosius I (ruled 379–95) issued a series of decrees outlawing paganism. Almost overnight the power of the Parthenon as a temple to Athene had been extinguished.

Reconsecrated as a Christian church and dedicated to Our Lady of Athens, the Parthenon was redesigned to fit the new religion. Arched windows were cut into walls and doors were knocked through, and, where the worshipper had once approached the *cella* from the east, an apse was built, while a bell tower was erected on the west. In time this tower would serve as minaret for, after the fall of Constantinople in 1453, Athens was conquered by the Turks. When, two centuries later, they were besieged by the Venetians (1687), the Turks chose to use the Parthenon as a munitions store. Perhaps they did not think that the Venetians would bombard so venerable a building. They were wrong. A direct hit caused a massive explosion, blowing out the centre of the Parthenon and leaving it in ruins.

Today those ruins have been carefully remodelled to create the broken shell of the once incomparable temple which has become a potent symbol of Athens and all Greece. Gazing on it, the viewer cannot but wonder at the power and ingenuity of the city state that built it. Yet, it would be well to remember the words of the historian Thucydides. Clear-eyed and down-to-earth, he recognized that much of Athens' seeming greatness was based upon a sham. Early in his history he wrote in words which were all too prescient and which seem deliberately calculated to contradict the rousing words of Pericles with which this book began:

> Imagine that Sparta became uninhabited, with only
> the foundations of its buildings still intact. As time
> passed, future generations would, I think, find it

Opposite Seen from Mount Lycabettus, the Parthenon still dominates the Athenian skyline, while at sea ships anchor off Piraeus.

hard to believe that it had ever been as powerful
as men said it was. For Sparta has no very striking
monuments or temples. But if the same were to
happen in Athens, you would think from what you
saw that the city had been twice as powerful as she
really is.[181]

Above The Greek mainland, the Aegean islands and the eastern
Greek world.

BLACK SEA   PAPHLAGONIA

BOSPHORUS

OLI
SULA

Lampsacus

ARDANELLES (HELLESPONT)

MOUNT TMOLUS
● Sardis

IONIA
● Ephesus

SAMOS × Mycale
●Miletus
●Didyma

Eurymedon ×

CARPATHUS

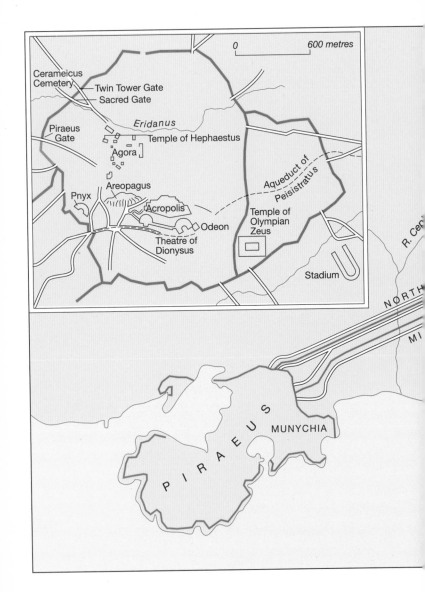

Above Athens in the fifth-century BC (inset) in the context of the
Long Walls and Piraeus.

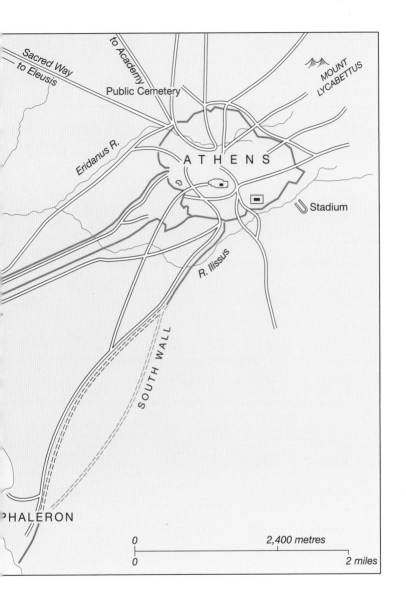

Sacred Way to Eleusis

to Academy

Public Cemetery

MOUNT LYCABETTUS

Eridanus R.

A T H E N S

Stadium

R. Ilissus

SOUTH WALL

PHALERON

0

0

2,400 metres

2 miles

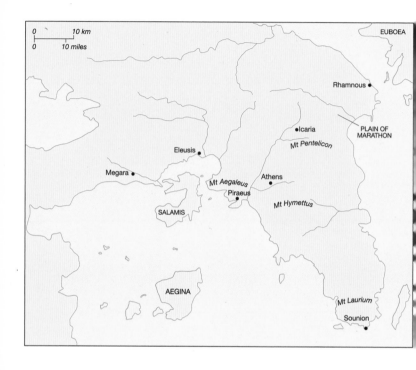

Above Attica and surrounding areas.

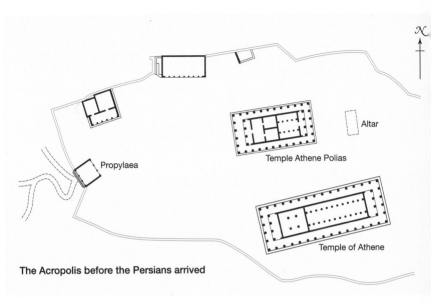

The Acropolis before the Persians arrived

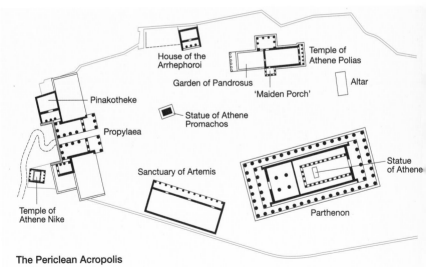

The Periclean Acropolis

Above The Acropolis.

Notes

1   Arguments rage about the date of the introduction of the
    Panathenaic ship: N.J. Norman, 'The Panathenaic ship',
    Archaeological News, vol. 12, 1983, pp. 41–3 argues convincingly
    for a later date; others, e.g. J.M. Mansfield, *The Robe of Athena
    and the Panathenaic Peplos*, Ph.D diss., University of California at
    Berkley, 1985, pp. 68–78, argue for an introduction after the
    battle of Salamis.

2   See I. Jenkins, *Greek Architecture and its Sculpture*, London, 2006, p. 27.

3   This (and the other quotations from Pericles' speech) comes
    from Thucydides (2.34 ff.). We have very little evidence about
    exactly how the particular public burial took place. I have based
    this reconstruction on references in Thucydides, on discussions
    about funeral rites contained in M. Alexiou's *The Ritual Lament in
    Greek Tradition* (second edn, 2002) and on the recent archaeology
    of ancient Athens' national cemetery, the so-called Demosion
    Sema.

4   Xenophon, *On Horsemanship*, 1.3.

5   Thucydides, 2.34.5.

6   Pausanias, 1.32.3.

7   Aeschylus, *Agamemnon*, 4.

8   Thucydides, 2.35.

9   Herodotus, 1.59; Aristotle, *The Constitution of Athens*, 16.

10 For more on the two-stade race and on the Olympic Games in
    general, see David Stuttard, *Power Games*, London, 2012.

11 Modern Glyfada.

12 Apollodorus, 3.14.1.

13 Characters associated with snakes or possessing snaky attributes
    are thought by some scholars to suggest *chthonic* gods or heroes
    (i.e. to be connected with the earth). Freudians, of course, may
    have other theories.

14 Apollodorus, 3.15.4. A fragmentary play by Euripides,
    Erechtheidai, first performed *c*.420 BC, also contains tantalizing
    details of the myth.

15 Pausanias, 1.26.7.

16 So writes Pausanias (1.22.5). Another version has Aegeus
    throwing himself from Cape Sounion (see Chapter 6).

17 Plutarch, *Life of Theseus*, 26 (Amazons); 35 (death). Plutarch's
    rationalizing account of the Minotaur episode is a masterly
    piece of interpretation.

18 Lycurgus, *Against Leocrates*, 84–7.

19 Thucydides, 1.126.

20 The statue mentioned here is presumed to be the olive-wood statue associated with Erechtheus.

21 Plutarch, *Life of Solon*, 26.

22 Any attempt to get at the truth is further impeded by the fact that, in the fifth century BC and later, Solon became thought of as a proto-democrat, and his reforms as early attempts at paving the way for full democracy.

23 This version of events is promoted, for example, in Plutarch, *Life of Solon*, 13.

24 Plutarch, *Life of Solon*, 1.

25 The 'Great Mysteries' were celebrated in the Attic month of Boedromion, corresponding to mid-September to mid-October; the 'Lesser Mysteries' took place in the month of Anthesterion, our mid-February to mid-March.

26 Plutarch, *Life of Theseus*, 20.

27 For a full consideration of the archaic Artemision see I. Jenkins 2006 (see note 2), pp. 56 ff.

28 See J. Neils, *Goddess and Polis*, Princeton, 1992, pp. 17 ff.

29 This and the following extract come from Thucydides, 6.56.

30 Thucydides, 2.36.

31 Herodotus, 5.62.

32 Herodotus, 5.63.

33 The nature of Athenian democracy is discussed in Chapter 3.

34 Herodotus, 5.72.

35 Herodotus, 5.73.

36 Xenophanes, fragment 3 (West).

37 Herodotus, 5.101–2.

38 Herodotus, 6.19.

39 The jury is (and will remain) out as to whether women were allowed to attend the theatre in Athens. The present author believes that they were not.

40 Herodotus, 6.21. In fifth-century BC Athens a skilled worker could expect to earn a drachma a day. For such a person, therefore, 1,000 drachmas is the equivalent of just under three years' wages.

41 Herodotus, 5.105.

42 Herodotus, 1.64.

43 They were transported to work in the oil fields of what is now southern Iraq. This episode and the subsequent account of Marathon can be found in Herototus, 6.101 ff.

44   Plutarch, *Life of Theseus*, 35.

45   Three hundred times the fine which Phrynichus the dramatist
      had been forced to pay a mere four years earlier.

46   Plutarch, *Life of Themistocles*, 5.

47   See, for example, J.R.Hale, *Lords of the Sea: The Triumph and
      Tragedy of Ancient Athens*, London, 2010, p. 20.

48   Herodotus, 7.5–6. He adds another reason: that imperial
      horticulturalists kept reminding Xerxes of the prospects of new
      shrubs and trees which might be found in Europe and brought
      back lovingly to grace the elaborately irrigated paradise gardens
      of Persia.

49   Herodotus, 7.184 puts it at 1,700,000 infantry and 80,000 cavalry.
      Modern estimates vary between 90,000 and 360,000 men.

50   Herodotus, 7.140.

51   Herodotus, 7.141.

52   Plutarch, *Life of Cimon*, 5.

53   Herodotus, 8.53.

54   Herodotus, 8.54.

55   Thucydides, 2.41.

56   Herodotus, 8.55

57   Herodotus, 8.65.

58   Aeschylus, *Persians*, 424–5.

59   Herodotus, 8.88.

60   Herodotus, 8.140a.

61   These coins can now be seen in the Acropolis Museum in
      Athens.

62   Herodotus, 8.144.

63   Lycurgus, *Against Leocrates*, 81. The so-called 'Oath of Plataea'
      has been the subject of much controversy, but to the present
      author there seems no conclusive reason for doubting its
      authenticity.

64   Herodotus, 9.120–1.

65   Herodotus, 9.120–1.

66   Such, at least, is the implication of the fact that on days when
      the Assembly was being held, 'policemen' ran through the
      Agora holding ropes which had been dipped in scarlet dye,
      shepherding reluctant citizens before them. Any tardy citizen
      whose tunic was found to have been marked by the dye was
      fined.

67   Aristotle, *Constitution of Athens*, 7.

68   Plutarch, *Life of Cimon*, 13.

69   Plutarch, *Life of Cimon*, 8.

70   Plutarch, *Life of Theseus*, 36.

71   Pausanias, 1.17.2–3.

72   Pausanias, 1.15.4.

73   Plutarch, *Life of Aristides*, 25.

74   Thucydides 1.98–9.

75   Herodotus, 9.120–1.

76   Plutarch, *Life of Cimon*, 17.

77   Such, at least, is the implication of Antiphon, 5.68.

78   Plutarch, *Life of Cimon*, 19.

79   Historians endlessly debate whether the Peace of Callias was
      ever in fact made. Its terms appear in the much later history of
      Diodorus Siculus (12.4).

80   Thucydides, 2.43.

81   See J. Neils, *Parthenon*, Cambridge, 2005, p. 52.

82   Pausanias, 10.10.1.

83   See, for example, M. Dillon and L. Garland, *Social and Historical
      Documents from Archaic Times to the Death of Alexandrer the Great*,
      Abingdon, 2010, p. 11.

84   Strabo, 9.1.12 and 9.1.16 and Pausanias, 8.41.9.

85   Vitruvius, *About Architecture*, 1.1.2 ff. Vitruvius, 7 praef 12
      mentions Ictinus' treatise, which he says Ictinus wrote with a
      colleague, Carpion. See Jenkins 2006 (note 2), p. 31.

86   Plutarch, *Life of Pericles*, 13.

87   Today most of the metopes are in a ruinous condition, and
      much of their detail has been lost. This description of them
      'as new' therefore contains an element of conjecture.

88   The west metopes, now in a particularly poor condition, can be
      seen in Athens' Acropolis Museum. None of the bronze fittings
      has, of course, survived, but, extrapolating from other such
      sculptures, the addition of shields etc can be assumed.

89   Aristophanes, *Knights*, 566.

90   It can be argued that there is nothing new in the choice of
      subject matter for the Parthenon metopes, most of which
      appears elsewhere on other temples throughout the Greek
      world. As we shall see, however, the way in which these themes
      are unified and explored elsewhere in other sculptures of the
      Parthenon suggests that Pheidias did indeed intend to link the
      theme of the victory of civilization over barbarism with Athens'
      own political and military successes.

91   Plutarch, *Life of Pericles*, 7.

92   Plutarch, *Life of Pericles*, 5.

93   Plutarch, *Life of Pericles*, 5.

94   Plutarch, *Life of Pericles*, 3.
95   Plutarch, *Life of Pericles*, 4.
96   T. Spawforth, The Complete Greek Temples, London, 2006, p. 70. Athens' annual revenue was 400 talents.
97   Plutarch, *Life of Pericles*, 14.
98   The name of Pericles' ostracised opponent was Thucydides, son of Milesias. I have deliberately not named him in the text, in order to avoid confusion with Thucydides the historian.
99   Thucydides, 2.65.
100 See Neils 2005 (note 81), pp. 272 ff.
101 Lucian, *The Cock*, 24.
102 Plutarch, *Moralia*, 499E; Dioscourides, *De Materia Medica*, 2.87.
103 Thucydides, 2.13.5. In 2013 a kg of gold was worth £36,350, making the value of the gold on Pheidias' statue £37,600,000.
104 Plutarch, *Life of Pericles*, 31.
105 Plutarch, *Life of Coriolanus*, 38.
106 Suetonius, *Caligula*, 57, see Stuttard 2012 (note 10), p. 212.
107 Plutarch, *Life of Pericles*, 31.
108 Hesiod, *Theogony*, 591–3.
109 Hesiod, *Works and Days*, 60 ff.
110 Spawforth 2006 (see note 96), p. 92.
111 See Neils 2005 (note 81), p. 286.
112 Jenkins 2006 (see note 2), p. 37.
113 It is debated whether wax or wash was indeed used in this way on ancient temples. See Jenkins 2006, p. 35.
114 Thucydides, 2.38.
115 The order of events followed here is that given by Neils 1992 (see note 28), p. 15.
116 The prizes here are taken from an Athenian inscription (*IG*II²2311) from around 370 BC.
117 For a consideration of the *pankration* and other sports, see Stuttard 2012 (note 10).
118 Plato, *Laws*, 7.815a.
119 Greek days ran from sunset to sunset, not from the arbitrary hour of midnight to midnight. The exact date of Athene's birthday (like so much) is contested. Was it the third day from the start or from the end of Hecatombeion? We just do not know.
120 Does this suggest more than one dedicatee? Or that it was named from the girls who wove the robe for Athene?
121 Plutarch, *Life of Pericles*, 12.
122 See Anton Powell, *Athens and Sparta*, London, 1988, pp. 60 ff.

123   Anton Powell, *Athens and Sparta*, London, 1988, p. 13.

124   Stuttard 2012 (note 10), pp. 24 ff.

125   See Neils 2005 (note 81), p. 230.

126   Inscriptions indicate that the pediments were sculpted between 438 and 432 BC. See Jenkins 2006 (note 2), p. 87.

127   The pedimental sculptures are now in a ruined state. The identification of their subject matter is based on a later description by Pausanias as well as on the drawings of Jacques Carrey who saw them in 1687 before their destruction at the hands of the Venetians.

128   The precise identity of these gods is open to dispute, as most are destroyed or ruined. See Neils 2005 (note 81), pp. 236 ff.

129   Apollodorus, *Library*, 1.6.1.

130   Herodotus, 7.141.

131   See Neils 2005 (note 81), p. 259 (note 146) and M. Korres, 'The architecture of the Parthenon', in P. Tournikiotis, *The Parthenon and its Impact on Modern Times*, Athens, 1994, fig. 8.

132   Homer, *Iliad*, 18, 478–608.

133   None of these metal fixings have survived, but the holes into which they were originally fixed are clearly visible.

134   See I. Jenkins, 'The Parthenon frieze and Perikles' cavalry of a thousand' in J. Barringer and J. Hurwit (eds), *Periklean Athens and its Legacy, Problems and Perspectives*, Austin, 2005, pp. 147–61.

135   Xenophon, *On Being a Good Cavalry Commander*, 3.2 ff.

136   Xenophon, *On Horsemanship*, 11.12

137   The horse was sacred to Poseidon, like the warships in which many Athenians rowed to victory.

138   See S. Moorhead's excellent article, 'Real life', on the heifers of the Parthenon frieze in the *British Museum Magazine* No. 72, 2012, p. 53.

139   Again, many of these attributes were attached in bronze or painted onto the marble.

140   First suggested by A.H. Smith, *A Catalogue of Sculpture in the Department of Greek and Roman Antiquities, British Museum*, vol. 1, London, 1892, p. 157; see Neils 2005 (note 81), p. 216.

141   Euripides, *Erechtheus*, fr. 370 in C. Collard, M.J. Cropp and K.H. Lee, *Euripides, Selected Fragmentary Plays*, vol. 1, Warminster, 1995.

142   Thucydides, 2.41.

143   Herodotus, 6.87 tells of an attack on this trireme by ships from Aegina.

144   Herodotus, 8.121.

145   There is some debate about the subject of this frieze. Some

say it showed Theseus hunting the Calydonian boar, but see I. Leventi in P. Schultz and R. von den Hoff (eds), *Structure, Image, Ornament: Architectural Sculpture in the Greek World. Proceedings of an International Conference Held at the American School of Classical Studies, 27–8 November 2004*, Oxford/Oakville, CT, 2009.

146   The temple of Athene measured 54 ft x 38 ft (16.4 m x 11.6 m) as opposed to the temple of Poseidon, whose proportions were 102 ft x 44 ft (31.15 m x 13.4 m).

147   Thucydides, 2.38.2.

148   Hermippus, fr. 63, found in Athenaeus, 1.27E–28A.

149   Neils 2005 (note 81), p. 60.

150   Here, just over thirty years later, the philosopher Socrates would be imprisoned and executed.

151   Such, at least, is the view of R. Carpenter in his controversial book, *The Architects of the Parthenon*, Michigan, 1970.

152   Plutarch, *Life of Pericles*, 13.

153   Pausanias, 1.20.6 ff.

154   Perhaps in 430 BC, the sanctuary of Artemis Brauronia was begun to the west of the Parthenon, which, when complete, would partially obscure the view of the Parthenon from the Propylaea.

155   Carpenter 1970 (see note 51), p. 139.

156   See Jenkins 2006 (note 2), p. 251 note 4.12, citing H. Goette, *Athens, Attica and the Megarid: An Archaeological Guide*, London and New York, 2001, p. 81.

157   The comic poet Cratinus gave this version of the myth in his lost *Nemesis*, whose plot is summarized by Eratosthenes, *Katasterismoi*, 25.

158   Pausanias, 33.2.

159   See W.B. Dinsmoor, *Proc. Am. Phil. Soc.*, vol. 80, 1939, pp. 132–3, 145, 152–3, 164; cf. *Athenian Archon List*, 1939, pp. 208–9.

160   Pausanias, 33.3–7.

161   It has even been suggested, somewhat unconvincingly given its proportions, that it was used as the original stage building (in Greek, *skene*, or 'tent') for the Theatre of Dionysus.

162   Vitruvius, 5.9.1.

163   M. McDonald and M. Valton (eds), *The Cambridge Companion to Greek and Roman Theatre*, Cambridge, 2007, pp. 208 ff.

164   Plutarch, *Life of Pericles*, 13. In fact, music had featured in the Panathenaic Games before Pericles. He merely increased its profile.

165   Euripides, *Medea*, 824 ff.

166 Thucydides, 2.52.

167 Thucydides, 2.44.

168 Thucydides, 2.31 lists 10,000 Athenians, 3,000 Potidaeans and 3,000 'resident aliens'.

169 The description of the plague and its effects is contained in Thucydides, 2.47–55.

170 Because of the way in which it is built to suit the terrain, scholars believe that the temple was built by Mnesicles, who overcame similar physical obstacles to construct the Propylaea. These obstacles, of course, would have had to be overcome by whoever the architect happened to be, and although it is less satisfying to admit ignorance, we cannot really know who built the temple of Athene Polias.

171 Pausanias, 1.26.7. Pausanias referred to the whole building as the Erechtheum, the name by which it is commonly called today.

172 Pausanias, 1.27.1.

173 This was not the only temple to bear the marks of Zeus' thunderbolt. At Olympia, too, such a mark was shown – supposedly the thunderbolt had been hurled this time to show Zeus' approval of Pheidias' statue of him. See Stuttard 2012 (note 10), p. 13.

174 Pausanias, 1.26.6.

175 Today they have acquired the name 'caryatids' thanks to a misunderstanding of Vitruvius, 1.1.5.

176 Pausanias, 1.27.7.

177 Thucydides, 5.89.

178 See, for example, Aristophanes' *Lysistrata*.

179 See M. Beard, *The Parthenon*, London, 2010, p. 150.

180 See D. Stuttard and S. Moorhead, *31 BC, Antony, Cleopatra and the Fall of Egypt*, London, 2012, pp. 134 ff.

181 Thucydides, 1.10.

Acknowledgements

The Parthenon and the statue which it housed were the product of a team of expert craftsmen. So, too, this book would not have been possible without the collaboration and encouragement of many inspirational and exceptional people, whom I should like warmly to acknowledge and thank here.

I am immensely grateful to Rosemary Bradley, Director of Publishing at the British Museum Press for commissioning the book; to Kate Oliver for producing it; to Bobby Birchall for its elegant design; to Sarah Derry for her sterling work as copy editor; to Katie Anderson for her picture research; to the British Museum's Department of Photography and Imaging for helping to provide such a cornucopia of stunning images; and to David Hoxley for his clear, crisp maps. My thanks, too, to the staff of the British School of Archaeology in Athens for their warm hospitality during my field trip to Attica while researching this book.

I have been fortunate on this, as on previous projects, to have had as my editor the wonderful Emma Poulter, whose serenity and efficiency I always much appreciate and whose good humour helps to make the process so enjoyable.

From an early stage, this book was championed by Sam Moorhead, with whom I co-wrote (*inter alia*) 'Riding to resurrection', an article about the gods on the Parthenon frieze for the *British Museum Magazine* (No. 62, Winter 2008). My thanks to him for his confidence in me, and for his indefatigable support throughout the writing process. Thanks, too, to my father-in-law, the sculptor Chris Hall, with whom I gave a gallery talk on the pediments in 2012, and whose explication of the techniques of his fifth-century BC colleagues I have found profoundly valuable.

I am particularly grateful to Ian Jenkins, the doyen of Parthenon studies, who with wit and patience, generosity of spirit and immense wealth of knowledge, has given so freely of his time, reading drafts, correcting errors and making what were always good suggestions. His belief in the project has been a constant inspiration, and any errors which remain embedded in the text are the result of my own intransigence.

Finally, I should like to thank my friends and family for their ongoing forbearance and encouragement: especially my mother, Kate, to whom this book is dedicated; and my wife EJ, whose patience is, indeed, that of a saint and whose friendship and support are the Acropolis upon which this *Parthenon* is built.

Index

Picture Credits

Page
2 British Museum 1841,B.1394
10 bpk | Bayerische Staatsgemäldesammlungen
12 British Museum 1805,0703.91
15 British Museum 1930,0417.1
19 Photo courtesy of the author
20 British Museum 1816,0610.43 (Block XLIV)
22 © The Acropolis Museum, Athens; photo: Socrates Mavromatis
24 British Museum 1853,0307.457. Bequeathed by Hon. Keppel Richard Craven
29 British Museum 1837,0609.54
32 British Museum 1850,0302.3
36 © The Acropolis Museum, Athens; photo: Socrates Mavromatis
40 British Museum 1907,1201.878
44 © The Acropolis Museum, Athens; photo: Socrates Mavromatis
46 British Museum 1866,0415.246. Donated by George Dennis
48 British Museum 1894,0331.20
51 Photo courtesy of the author
56 Photo courtesy of the author
63 British Museum 1897,1231.7. Bequeathed by Sir Augustus Wollaston Franks
67 British Museum 1849,0620.12
71 British Museum 1882,0704.1
76 British Museum 1836,0224.13
79 British Museum 1865,0103.14
81 British Museum 1889,0522.1.A1
85 British Museum 1875,0309.24
90 British Museum 1866,0805.2. Donated by Thomas Sharpe Smith
93 Photo courtesy of the author
96 Photo courtesy of the author
102 British Museum 1816,0610.73
104 Photo courtesy of the author
111 British Museum 1846,0629.45
116 Photo courtesy of the author
119 British Museum 1816,0610.12
127 Photo © Gary Layda by courtesy of Wesely Paine, Metro Board of Parks and Recreation
131 British Museum 1864,0220.18
134 British Museum 1856,1213.1
137 British Museum 1816,0610.397
138 Photo: akg-images / Peter Connolly
143 British Museum 1816,0610.81
144 © The Acropolis Museum, Athens; photo: Socrates Mavromatis
146 British Museum 1816,0610.86
152 British Museum 1816,0610.99
154 British Museum
158 © Birmingham Museums Trust
162 British Museum 1816,0610.42 (Block XLIII)
166 British Museum 1816,0610.18 (Block IV)
168 British Museum 1816,0610.19 (Block V)
172 Photo courtesy of the author
174 British Museum 1816,0610.128
176 © Packard Humanities Institute
180 Photo courtesy of the author
183 Photo courtesy of the author
188 British Museum 1820,0513.2
193 British Museum 1948,1015.3
201 Photo courtesy of the author
204 British Museum 1816,0610.161
207 Photo courtesy of the author
211 © The Acropolis Museum, Athens; photo: Socrates Mavromatis
212 British Museum 2012,5007.23. Donated by Ita Rennie
217 © The Acropolis Museum, Athens; photo: Socrates Mavromatis
Maps Courtesy of Technical Art Services